STAINED GLASS
A Basic Manual

STAINED GLASS

A Basic Manual

Barbara and Gerry Clow

Photographs by Gerry Clow
Diagrams by Jack Trompetter

BOSTON　　　　　Little, Brown and Company　　　　　TORONTO

FIRST EDITION
T02/76

Library of Congress Cataloging in Publication Data

Clow, Barbara.
    Stained glass.

    (Little, Brown crafts series)
    Bibliography: p.
    1. Glass painting and staining. I. Clow,
Gerry, joint author. II. Title.
TT298.C56   748.5'028   75-28103
ISBN 0-316-14753-2

Published simultaneously in Canada
by Little, Brown & Company (Canada) Limited

PRINTED IN THE UNITED STATES OF AMERICA

To Louis Comfort Tiffany and my two sons, Tommy and Matthew

The Little, Brown Crafts Series is designed and published for the express purpose of giving the beginner — usually a person trained to use his head, not his hands — an idea of the basic techniques involved in a craft, as well as an understanding of the inner essence of that medium. Authors were sought who do not necessarily have a "name" but who thoroughly enjoy sharing their craft, and all their sensitivities to its unique nature, with the beginner. Their knowledge of their craft is vital, although it was realized from the start that one person can never teach all the techniques available.

The series helps the beginner gain a sense of the spirit of the craft he chooses to explore, and gives him enough basic instruction to get him started. Emphasis is laid on creativity, as crafts today are freed from having to be functional; on process, rather than product, for in the making is the finding; and on human help, as well as technical help, as so many prior teaching tools have said only "how" and not "why." Finally, the authors have closed their books with as much information on "next steps" as they could lay their hands on, so that the beginner can continue to learn about the craft he or she has begun.

Gerald Clow

Thanks to the blown glass and stained glass I loved in Saginaw, Michigan, as a child.

Thanks to Mr. and Mrs. Sherman Smith of Seattle, Washington, for teaching me about house restoration.

Thanks to the pre-earthquake streets of San Francisco.

Thank you, Patrick Curran, Stephen Schneider, Rodger Chamberlain, Jack Trompetter, and Gerry Clow for advice and contributions for this book. Jack Trompetter contributed all the illustrations and did a magnificent job, and Gerry Clow did the photography for the book.

Barbara Clow

Contents

Introduction

Five Things to Know before Beginning

What Is Stained Glass?

Most people think of one of two things when you say "stained glass": either the medium itself (the production of lamps, windows, boxes, pendants, jewelry, candle sconces, and an endless list of two- and three-dimensional objects designed to let light through one side and delight the viewer on the other) or they think of the glass itself. This is what we will discuss here.

"Stained glass" is also called *colored* or *art glass*. It is made with a variety of metal oxides (selenium, manganese, chromium, copper salts) and is produced primarily in sheet form in factories in Europe and the United States. Stained glass can also mean "glass which has been stained." *Stains,* which give "stained glass" its popular name, are chemical compositions made primarily of silver nitrate, which when heated in a kiln penetrates and fuses with the base glass. Glass is also *"painted,"* with ground glass and oxides, which are fired onto the glass in a kiln and fuse with the surface of the glass. Stains last as long as the glass they are in, while paints will chip and deteriorate, as old cathedral windows will testify.

Stained (colored, art) glass comes in three categories:

Antique glass

This is the oldest form of glass, and thus the name *antique*. It is made by a glassblower, who forms a cylinder, cutting it down the side and reheating the cylinder until it slowly splays down onto a flat surface, making a sheet. Sheets are limited to approximately 32 by 48 inches in size, because that is the size of cylinder a glassblower is capable of handling. Antique glass is brilliant, being made of the best metal oxides (the same glass is also used for making bottles, decanters, and art pieces), and is full of beautiful imperfections or variations, such as bubbles (unintentional), *seeds* (tiny bubbles, caused by gases still trapped in an underfired batch of glass), *reams* or warps, and varying thicknesses, all of which create varying light intensity. *Flashed antique*, which is made by dipping a bubble of light-colored antique glass into a strong, brilliant color (such as red, blue, or green over clear or yellow), is a variation of antique, popular with craftsmen who etch into glass; it also varies in intensity, with occasional swirls, owing to the irregularity of the "dip" or "flash."

Three kinds of glass: two samples of antique on the left; two cathedrals of different texturing in the middle; and two opalescents on the right.

Antique also comes as *clear antique* and *streaky antique*. Clear antique is no longer made: it is the old window glass you find in colonial or early nineteenth-century homes and once in a while in an old barn, waiting for you to rescue it and give it a new life. Old clear antique has streaks, lines and bubbles, and is wonderfully irregular in thickness, giving a dappled vision of the outside world. Streaky antique is made two ways: either two colors are swirled together in one pot or, as in flashed glass, only the applied glass is twirled on in stripes, which become streaky when the bubble is blown into a cylinder. The result in either case is Hollywood glass, perfect for optimistic skies and glorious sundowns. Enjoy.

Antique is made in France, Germany, and England, and in one company in America, the Blenko Glass Company of Milton, West Virginia, where the public is welcome to come watch the glassblowers work. Handmade and made of the best oxides, antique is the most expensive of glasses. Yet it is the undisputed prize of glass artists, used exclusively by some, or else as highlights, to contrast with lesser-quality glass, by others.

This is the traditional use of flashed antique glass: etching. This 6" x 8" piece, called "Art Nouveau Lady," was etched on blue flashed-on-white glass by Patrick Curran of Florence, Mass., in 1974.

Cathedral glass

This glass is a product of the Industrial Age. During the latter half of the nineteenth century, some glass was made by machine. Some glaziers refer to it as "commercial" glass. Since it is not handmade and is made of cheaper oxides, some refrain from using it altogether. It is often called "bathroom" glass. Yet cathedrals, especially the older imported European ones, have made many a majestic window. This glass is made in the same way as clear sheet glass: glass is poured in its molten state out onto a large metal table and either smooth or rough rollers texture the surface, on one side or both. Granite, satin, hammered, and double rolled are some of the kinds of names cathedral glass has. Once textured, the sheet of glass (now 7 by 4 feet, no longer limited in size) travels automatically through a long *annealing* oven, which brings the glass down to air temperature slowly (the sheet of antique glass goes through a similar oven).

Cathedral glass serves several purposes. At best, it gives windows a deliberate texture antique glass could not. Many of our fellow glaziers use cathedral for such details as water in a window scene. Some American cathedrals are brilliant enough in color to compete with antique, although they still have the machine-made texture, which interferes with the passage of light. To the nineteenth-century studios, cathedral glass filled a need for a less expensive glass, readily available in large quantities, which could be used for painting, leaving the more expensive antiques as colorful highlights in church windows. In this country, you'll find late-nineteenth-century domestic windows full of European cathedrals, which are more muted and a more softly-textured glass than American cathedrals and beautiful in comparison to rondels, crackle glass (another form of antique), and opalescents.

Opalescent glass

This is the American entry into the glass field, originated in the days when Louis Tiffany and his contemporary, John La Farge, were entering the stained glass business in New York City in the 1880's. They were experimental designers who wanted a glass which they could use for highlighting, for giving depth and detail to landscape. If you were going to block out the light, it might as well be with the glass and not with paint, which Tiffany found repugnant to his design sensibilities. Both men are credited with "discovering" opalescent glass. Basically they, and later Tiffany alone, subsidized several Long Island and New Jersey glassmakers, who began making a new kind of pot glass with soda ash thrown in, making it smoky or chalky; bright color oxides were added to this one pot of molten glass, and the glassmaker swirled them in irregular streaks throughout the sheet as he poured out the glass. There was no limit other than personal taste or preference to the number of colors which could be added. The result was sheets of very elaborate, multicolored opaque art glass. Later, a differentiation was made between *opal* (clear-based) and *opalescent* (milky-based) glasses.

Tiffany spent most of his inheritance subsidizing his glass works. Later, they were to supply the opalescent for his now-famous Tiffany shades, which became the rage once the electric bulb was invented. Companies were to spring up—three in number—which began making new opalescents, some of which he used in his studios. They started in Indiana, West Virginia, and Ohio, where the natural gas used in firing the glass kilns was plentiful.

Finally, as valuable accessories to the business of stained glass, there are such things as *rondels,* spun, flat disks of antique glass, round in shape; *jewels,* either cut or pressed in a mold, also made of antique glass; *beveled glass,* pieces of thick clear glass with the edges beveled at a 45-degree angle for a prismatic effect, and available in geometric or curved shapes; and *dalles de verre,* slabs of glass roughly 2 by 6 by 8 inches in dimension, developed in France during this century and also made at the Blenko factory. These *dalles de verre* are used whole to make monumental windows for to-day's architecture or cut up by the hobbyist into faceted, irregular nuggets and joined with others by cement or epoxy.

These are a few of the jewels and rondels we use in our shop. The lower level has three rondels, the largest a cut cylinder bottom from Blenko Glass Company, a 4" x 5" imported beveled piece, and a larger amber rondel. The upper jewels vary from an antique turn signal (Model T Ford era), two round clear colored jewels, which come with wide lips for leading; two pressed jewels (in a mold); and a square (milky) and large round (purple) jewel, both handcut in the 1880's.

How Do You Do It?

This is the question this book is meant to answer. I bring it up now in order to introduce you to the new twist (which I will explain in detail later) we have added to a very tradition-bound craft.

Techniques for making stained glass have changed very little over the years. Tiffany introduced his new glass and began using copper instead of lead to join his pieces of cut glass together. And electricity has made soldering easier, with lightweight soldering irons re-placing the torch-fired copper-element irons of the past.

Yet fundamentally, the methods, from designing to cutting to laying out and leading up, have remained the same for centuries. This has been the "lost" art, guarded in closed studios around the country, carried on by strict apprenticeships, and rarely opened up to public (and/or experimental) scrutiny.

In this book Barbara introduces something fundamentally new to the stained glass business. She began working with glass as the busy mother of two boys and the designer for a jewelry company in California. She found that making designs, making copies of them, and cutting out templates as cutting guides was too time-consuming, and it also alienated her from her original cartoon. She wanted to work directly from her original drawing. With the aid of the electric light bulb (something our ancestors did not have) she was able to light up a glass cutting surface from underneath and thus illuminate the cartoon and the glass laid over it. She called this method the *Light Box Technique,* and found that she could cut out a window in half the time it took traditional glaziers. This process of working right from the design and checking each piece as she went along was very tactile and spontaneous as well, something she valued highly in a craft. Paper templates were not her idea of tactile pleasure.

We have since found out that the Museum School of Boston also teaches this method of cutting glass; perhaps there are other schools and other glaziers using it. However, this is the first time it has been documented in a printed book.

The other methods of making lamps and windows, which have been carried on for years, will be covered in the rest of the book just as they have always been taught. In a few cases, we'll introduce some new variations on old techniques; for example, in etching or making mold lamps.

Who Else Is Doing It and What Are They up to?

This book gives you a look at the original designs and methods of one glazier, and a passing look at the designs and methods of four other glaziers working near us in New England. There are dozens of other people whose work is worthy of publication whom we could have invited into the book.

We are working at a time of enormous national interest in stained glass. I worked as the crafts columnist for the *Boston Globe* for two years, at a time when crafts were beginning to boom. Pottery, weaving, woodwork, silversmithing: each had its own cult, its own heroes and followers, and all were being widely bought. Blown glass, first emerging from the kilns of a few pioneers in the crafts movement in the mid-1960's, hit the public eye by the early 1970's. Last in line was stained glass, held back by lack of knowledge of technique and supply, and shrouded in the mystique that it was a "lost" art.

28" laburnum shade, by Bauer and Cobel Studios, Champaign, Ill., 1974

I did not realize how large an upsurge there was going on outside our own pocket of business until we began this book. It forced us to travel and ask more questions.

10

We heard of a group of younger glaziers in Cleveland who had underbid a traditional studio for a church job and were busy making the windows in a warehouse. We met and saw stained glass craftspeople in towns throughout the Midwest and heard of others at the Rhinebeck Fair in New York this summer. We saw the incredible fine-lined lamps of Sandy Cresswell, of Santa Barbara, hanging in the halls of the Kokomo Glass Company. We heard of the Bauer and Coble Studios in Champaign, Illinois, reputed to be making Tiffany lampshade reproductions, finely crafted, with wax-cast reproduction bases, selling at a fair price. (Bob Bauer, one of the founders, holds a Ph.D. in Chemistry from the University of Illinois; because of the job market, he switched fields and has found a good response to his new business.) We see ads nearly each week in *The New York Times* for stained glass windows selling in junkyards for high prices, when only a few years ago you could buy them for very little. Restaurants and bars are full of stained glass now, and advertising in the media slips lamps and windows into their ads all the time. Handmade Houses and Woodstock Handmade Houses, which brought to the public new design sense toward building one's own house, are both full of original stained glass works. Upon returning home this fall, we began sending for catalogues from suppliers. The numbers of both catalogues and suppliers have increased each month, as have glass journals, which now include *Glass Art Magazine,* only in its third year.

My first window — a 12" x 10" panel, titled "Midwestern Dream"

Thus it is with enormous pride and some fear and trepidation that we begin our book. We have to work hard at our studio to stand up to our competition. Yet for a motivated beginner, this is a time when there are a growing market, increasing suppliers, and others' work around to stimulate his or her own. Keep your eyes open, not only to old lamps and windows, as Barbara suggests, but to new people working.

Being a Beginner

This to me is an important topic. This whole book is saturated with ideas and ways for the so-called "beginner" to begin. But to be that person, you would have to have what Zen calls a "beginner's mind," basically a head cleared of all subjective, personal thoughts and ideas. You'd have to be able to put yourself totally into Barbara's hands.

This, of course, is not always possible. People are never predictable. So I'll speak briefly on the unpredictable, yet predictable, sides of beginners.

Eighteen months ago I was a beginner. I began by feeling that everything Barbara told me was only what she herself thought. I did not see the experiments she had tried in forming her opinions. So, bravely, I decided to make a panel my own way. I drew a pencil sketch, a scene of a landscape with a house and a yellow rondel for a sun. I did not fill in or blacken the lines to allow for the thickness of lead. I grabbed the best-looking but worst-cutting glass in the studio, a piece of British streaky glass, for my sky. I tried to cut a perfect circle out of the sky, without breaking the rest of the sheet. The sheet shattered into four or five pieces, and de facto I was given lead lines in places where my design did not ask for them.

I continued. Wanting to complete the job that afternoon, I cut the purple glass for my house as I went along, improvising. Miraculously, I put all these little pieces together, after about an hour of them popping up and sliding under each other and the lead as I exerted pressure. After a few hours' work, I had my 10 by 12 inch panel: a bit lopsided, with weird fissures which I hoped the viewer would think were intended to be there. I was not too happy, but the puttying process cheered me up a lot. I was genuinely surprised at the polishing quality of putty, which caused an increase in light and softened the lead and solder joints to a smooth dull gray finish.

From this experience, I gained respect for doing things right. I vowed to make a correct cartoon the next time, to watch out for impossible glass cuts, and to putty the panel before I judged its merits and showed it to the public, as Barbara had suggested.

Barbara conceded that she, too, had approached glass this way. The "first window" she proudly displayed was actually preceded by her "first panel," which no longer exists. I thought back, too, to our apprentice Jim, who last winter struggled to make his first panel. He took a daring design, a star with long daggers of glass, easily breakable, hard to cut, which would buckle easily under pressure, and it took him four times the normal time to put it together.

An urge in the beginner, in any medium, is to express himself or herself. Unless you have the discipline from another medium, you'll tend to jump in, get your feet wet, and often drown. As Arnold Palmer says, learn to hit the ball far, then learn how to control it. Take this as a natural impulse. Accept it, and learn to try harder at the other side of the craft, not the romantic, "express yourself" side, but the classic, "do it correctly" side. Somewhere between the two you'll find yourself, your voice, your visual style.

Now, after eighteen months, I am just beginning to feel like a beginner. I've had time to chase away my preconceptions, which were my wonderings at Barbara's techniques and design sense. I've learned to appreciate her designs, her decisions, and the work of others. Once I accepted my limitations, I was much happier. I've learned to soak in what others have done or said; I'm open to experimenting, to learning many techniques and approaches before I decide on my own. To be a beginner, to my mind, is to learn to let glass speak to me and not me to it.

Finally, part of being a beginner is realizing the years it will take to call yourself a master. For me, that was a happy realization. Coming from the instant-pudding society, I was glad to find something inviolate, whose standards have remained the same for centuries—something to measure up to, which is manually hard but very satisfying.

This Book

By now you have learned a bit about us, the authors, and the techniques and sensibilities we are promoting.

A word should be said, before we begin, about why this book is written as it is.

We began by writing about materials and techniques. Out at the studio, way last January, we took stacks of pictures with a hand-held camera. We were jumping in, getting our feet wet as usual, and drowning a bit.

The book needed more direction and control. This involved the two of us deciding on a course of dual action. Many heated hours and days went into the (newly married) authors' ironing out important points, as to who was boss (neither of us), which pictures we should use, how they should relate to the text, and where the text should go, what it should say.

After long hours of writing, Barbara evolved her thinking to the point where she decided a program learning book was needed. Much control and encouragement is needed in doing work with glass, and whereas a potter can give you an idea and you can adapt it to your own hand and kickwheel, with glass you needed designs, cartoons, directions. Barbara began designing projects, and I was pleased to find them to be her best designs yet. She had made designs to encourage, to urge people to push the medium, to show them what could be done, not just what has already been done, and in the process she made very beautiful projects.

After struggling with photos, we gave up the on-site shots and set up a photography studio in our upstairs room. A tripod and lights let us shoot night and day, and let me get the depth of field without juggling the image. I learned how to move with the iron master, and the photos were done.

This book, then, is the struggle of two people in a year of thinking, evolving, and resolving. We are two glaziers working in an island of sorts. We work alone, while hearing of others working far off. We present our work, our ideas, our solutions to problems which bothered us, knowing full well that there are others out there with different solutions, different ideas and work habits. We hope that our solutions, and the way we express them, will be a good start for a beginner, and that Barbara's designs and cutting technique will spur you on in your investigations of glass.

Chapter One

Leading up a Simple Panel

You are ready to begin working with glass. We are going to start you out with a small panel. The techniques you will need to learn in order to execute this panel are simply explained, but these techniques take considerable time to master before you can be called really skilled. The techniques in the first chapter that teach how to make "stained" or "leaded" glass are designed for efficiency and accuracy. Modern labor costs are very high, and skill and speed have become a necessity.

In order to begin, you will have to establish a suitable workspace and purchase minimal materials and tools. Your commitment to glass can exist on many possible levels. You may wish to be a beginning hobbyist. You may wish to make an ambitious window or lamp for your own home. You may wish to become a stained glass artist. Whatever your aim, you must have at least the bare minimum of workspace and tools and materials. We can't possibly emphasize enough the importance of these first suggestions.

Glass is messy and can be dangerous. It is often frustrating, and you must begin fully prepared to cope with it. Your minimal workspace can be an old wooden table. The table must be sturdy, because you'll pound nails into it, and it must be level, so that you can be accurate. The table must not be in the middle of a high traffic area or be used for any other purpose. Your child, your mate, or your cat will not appreciate little slivers of glass in their feet. I've seen friends with high aptitude for glass work try to learn on the table they eat from, and they have failed. I've seen apprentices who seemed to possess no special abilities who've learned very quickly in our properly prepared studio.

Set up your worktable. As in the diagram on the right, nail two pieces of wood about 2 feet long and 1 inch by 2 inches to one corner of the table at right angles. If you are right-handed, set it up so that you'll push into the corner made by the wood on your right side. If you are left-handed, do the opposite. Your table is ready for work.

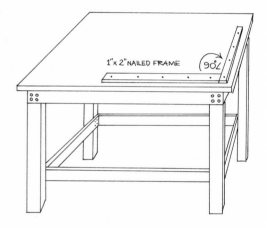

A stained glass worktable

Materials

You will have problems getting materials because of the complexity of the American market. In the appendix at the end of the book you'll find a partial list of suppliers that will be most helpful in the eastern United States. A basic understanding of the American market system might be the most help to you in the beginning. The primary source of any material or tool is the manufacturer or importer. The manufacturer or importer sells only to buyers of large quantity. These buyers are large studios, who use everything they buy themselves, or they are retailers, who mark things up and resell again. Sometimes the manufacturer or importer will maintain a retail outlet for buyers of small quantities, and often they are happy to allow people to tour their facilities. Most of the time you will buy from the retailers, who are in business to serve the hobbyist and beginner. Do not be afraid to call on the factories and importers and ask to buy or tour the premises. But do not be hurt if they put you off, because their average customer buys a minimum of five hundred dollars' worth or more. You will find the retailers by looking in the *Yellow Pages* under "Stained and Leaded Glass," studying our Appendix, which attempts to help you deal with various suppliers, and asking your local craft store person or hardware person. Your local department store may have an extensive craft section. When you start looking for supplies you may be tempted to buy a kit. This is extremely inadvisable, because the instructions are generally poor and misleading, the patterns are often faulty, the tools and supplies are poorly chosen, and you just don't know whom or what you are relying on.

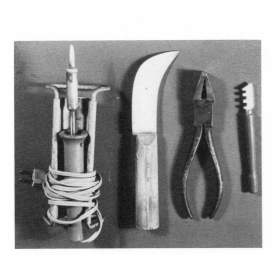

Basic tools

You will need to purchase a soldering iron, a few glass cutters, a pair of grozing pliers, oleic acid, soldering paste, whiting, glazing putty, a few strips of H-calm lead (pronounced "came") and two strips of U-calm lead, and a pound of solder. Those of you who are far from supplies may consult the Appendix to obtain things you need by mail.

Your soldering iron is your most crucial tool, and we recommend the Esico 60-watt iron. This iron can handle almost any situation with leaded and copper foil work. It is durable, inexpensive, small and light. It does not have to be "tinned" while you're working with it. Keep a wet sponge nearby as you work and wipe the iron off periodically. The manufacturer recommends coating the iron with soldering paste, or flux (which is any material which causes two metals of differing chemical compositions to adhere to each other), after a day's work and melting solder all over the tip. That is what "tinning" means. Some of the older irons have to be tinned frequently while working.

You can obtain steel glass cutters from your hardware store. They are available with steel or wooden handles but the wooden cutters are easier on your hand. The steel-handled cutters have a ball on the end of the handle for tapping, which we've found to be less accurate than tapping with the steel teeth on the wooden-handled cutter. Do not get into sharpening your cutters — it is very difficult and will not save you much money. Also, you may damage valuable glass with a home-sharpened cutter. Buy two or three cutters for a starter.

You can get grozing pliers from your local stained glass supplier. You will use the grozers to trim edges after you have cut pieces of glass, and they are essential.

You can order oleic acid, which is a flux, by the pint from your druggist, or you can get it by the ounce from your stained glass supplier. (You may find it is cheaper from your druggist.)

Buy glazing putty from your stained glass supplier. Glass putty is entirely different from common window putty. If you can get it ready-made, buy a small quantity, because you'll soon make your own. If you can't get it, make your own according to the instructions at the end of Chapter Two.

You'll need whiting, which is an adhesive compound, to polish your panel. You will find it at your hardware store, from your stained glass supplier, or from a local potter.

Glass

You might be wise to start out with scraps of clear glass, usually obtained free from your hardware store. You will find a limited selection of glass at the stained glass supplier's store. If you start with stained glass be sure to read the descriptions of various types of glass in our Introduction. Ask your supplier what type of glass it is you are buying and get him to tell you as much as he knows about it. Refer to Chapter Two for special problems with each type of glass. If you do start with stained glass, select light colors this time. In that way you will avoid the need for a light table or box.

Lead

Your stained glass supplier is your only source. Buy a half-dozen small-size H-calm and two U-calms. A lead calm is a six-foot-long strip of H- or U-shaped lead designed for leading glass. Calms have been made the same way for centuries. In the illustration you will notice the many types and sizes of lead available. Some beginners get the idea that they should pick out thick calm in order to cover up their errors. This is a mistake. The bigger calm is specially designed for big windows and various design problems. In big windows, underneath the wide calm lies a perfectly cut window. A badly cut window will bow in and out of shape even if you can't see it do so, because the wide calm covers the imperfections. You should use only thin calm in a small panel.

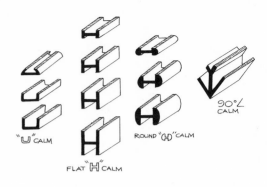

Lead calm

Solder

Solder is composed of 60 percent tin and 40 percent lead. You will melt the solder with the soldering iron over the lead calm in order to fuse the joints. Get one pound of 60/40 solder. Do not buy acid core solder because the flux in the acid core is unnecessary and will work against the oleic acid.

You have your basic materials.

The Cartoon

The pattern for a leaded panel or a leaded window, or for copper foil work and lamps is called a *cartoon*. A *design* is a working drawing done in pencil or ink and it becomes a cartoon when all the lines are blacked in 1/16 inch thick. The accuracy of the cutting of each

The leaded panel

piece of glass is totally dependent upon the accuracy of the cartoon. After you have finished cutting your glass you will use your cartoon again in order to assemble your panel. We stress the accuracy and beauty of the cartoon because the method we use is totally dependent upon the perfection of the cartoon. The beauty and artistic success of stained glass is the result of beautiful lines and colors. Often we hang up a finished cartoon for a few days to see if it stands alone as a nice pen-and-ink drawing.

The Panel

Let's look at it. (See page 25.) Unlike many beginning stained glass projects, our first design is not geometrical. Geometrical designs are easy to cut and hard to lead up, and they don't teach you very much about cutting or leading up. You may wish to start with your own design. If so, check the section on difficult cuts (page 55) and try to avoid difficult cuts at first. Also remember to lead in your pencil lines 1/16 inch thick. This line allows for lead, putty, and imperfections. The illustration of lead in glass might help you to imagine what goes on. You can black in the lines of a cartoon with a felt-tip pen.

Most glaziers do not use this method for leadwork. Instead, two cartoons are made up. They cut out all the pattern pieces of one cartoon within the 1/16 lines. They cut each piece of glass around each pattern and assemble the window over the second cartoon. This process

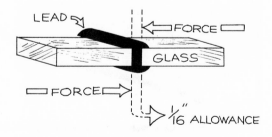

Glass fitting into lead calms

is time-consuming, leaves more room for inaccuracies, and, most seriously, makes leadwork into puzzle assembly instead of the tactile creation of a design. (There are situations where pattern pieces are used, and they will all be covered later.) Cutting directly over the cartoon does require demanding cutting skill initially, but it is very much like learning to play the piano properly on the very first exercise.

Cutting glass

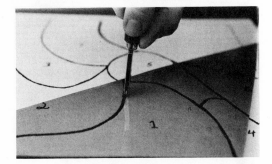

Cutting glass

Light Box

Learning to Cut Glass

Don't be afraid of the glass. Start with scrap glass and play with it. Examine the two photos and the photo sequence at left to get a feel for it. Notice how the cutter is held between the second and third fingers and the thumb. The main pressure is exerted downward from the second and third fingers gripping the cutter with the thumb. Try not to press the top of the cutter into the V of your fingers because you can get a bad blister there. You will probably have a tendency to press too hard—you are pressing too hard if you are making a deep scratch into the glass and slivers are flying up. Those of you who do not already wear glasses may wish to wear safety goggles if you tend to cut close to your face. If you press firmly but not hard, your cutter should sound like a skating blade cutting across freshly sprayed ice on a crisp winter day. Your cutter should leave a tiny white line and not a slashed ditch. Never rerun the cutter over a score line, because you will accomplish nothing and you'll wreck your cutter. The wheel of the cutter must be *exactly* on the inside of the cartoon line. You *can* be absolutely accurate. Cutting takes concentration, and one should not cut continuously for more than two hours. You will be very slow at first, but if you're accurate, you've made it more than halfway.

Once you have gotten a basic feel for cutting, you are ready to begin work on the enclosed panel. In the photo sequence you will notice that light glass is used. Normally light and dark glass would be used. The dark glass would be cut on a light table. A photo of a light box is given because you can make one if you selected glass too dark to see through unaided. Otherwise, follow along on the photo sequence with light glass.

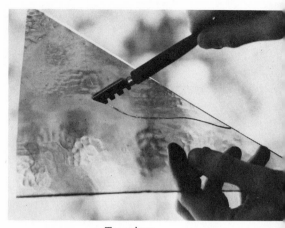

Tapping

Cutting the First Piece

In the photo sequence, piece 1 is being cut. Notice in the first photo how accurately the cutting wheel is

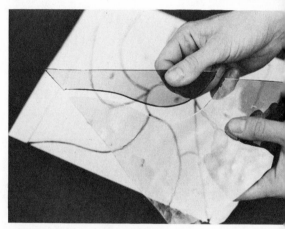

Separation

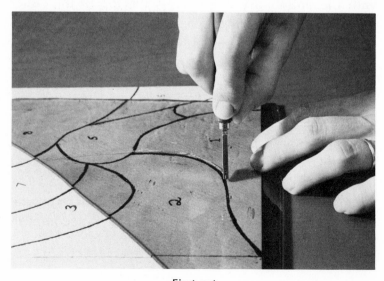

First cut

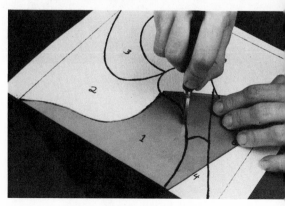

Second cut of piece #1

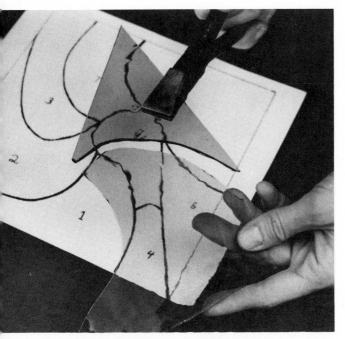

Snapping with grozers

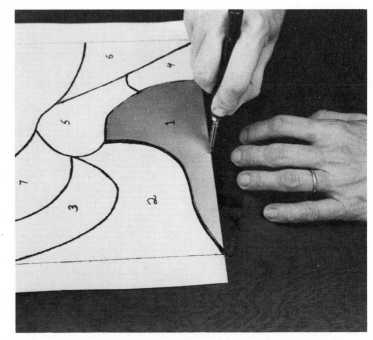

Straight cut

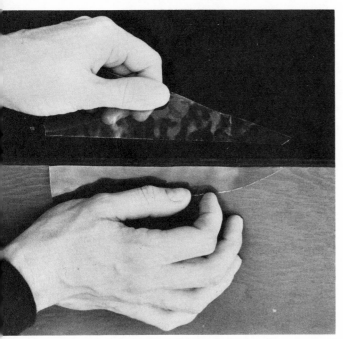

Snapping off table

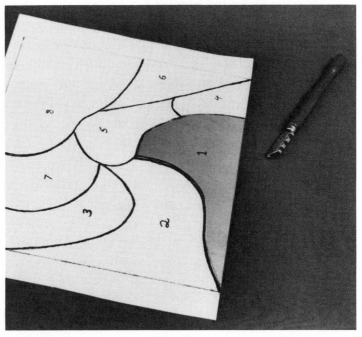

The piece

scoring the glass along the inside line of piece 1. The line caused by the cutter is the *score line.* In the second photo the piece is being *tapped* on the backside of the score line. The piece is being held up to the light so that the score line can be seen through the glass, and so that the emerging *break line* can be seen. The break line will *always* follow the score line exactly if the score line is tapped accurately and thoroughly. In the third photo the glass is being separated after the score line has been tapped completely and the break is finished. Gentle but firm pulling will accomplish this. You might have to tap it a bit more if the glass doesn't separate easily. In the fourth photo the second cut of piece 1 is being done. Notice again the accuracy of the cutting. In the fifth photo the second cut is being snapped off with the grozers in one hand after the score line has been tapped. In the sixth photo the last cut is being done. It is a straight cut and the easiest cut of the three. Always make the hardest cut first. In the seventh photo the straight cut is being done and is being *snapped off* the table edge. It's fun. Glass usually obeys the rules.

Cut the rest of your pieces following the principles just outlined. Place them all on their respective places on the cartoon, as in the last photo, and check them for accuracy. Label the pieces according to the cartoon numbers, and you're ready for leading up. When you were cutting your pieces, a few of you who did use stained glass may have cut some thick glass. Check the thickest edges to make sure that they will fit into your lead calm. If you happen to have any edges that will not fit, you will have to recut that section out of a thinner piece of glass and save the thick piece for *foiling* later.

Leading up

Leading up is like rebuilding a VW engine: if you complete each step correctly, there is no way you can go wrong. But if you do one small step incorrectly, the engine will be useless. Exactly the same analogy applies to our panel. If each piece is perfectly cut, and if you work each piece perfectly into position over its corresponding piece in the cartoon, the lead lines will be exactly over the cartoon lines, and your panel will be perfect.

You begin each assembly job by stretching the lead you will use. Lead comes from the factory extruded into shape, but it is not stretched out to its full length; therefore, you will be able to straighten it out just before use. Two people can stretch lead easily if each grabs an end in a pair of pliers or grozers and gently pulls the strip until they feel a little "snap" in the lead. Or one person can step on one end with the heel of a hard shoe or boot, grip the other end of the strip in pliers or grozers, and pull. No problem. A strip of small lead "gives" about six inches.

Ready to assemble your panel, you begin by cutting two pieces of U-calm lead for the edges of the panel and placing them in your table frame. Simply cut them the length of your cartoon side, allowing for the corner. You will be assembling your panel into that corner under force. Check the photo sequence (page 32) for the proper use of the lead knife and note that all the pieces

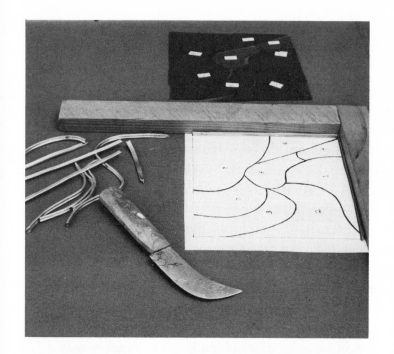
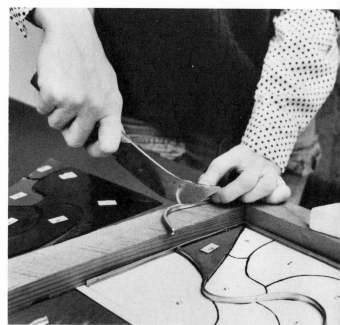
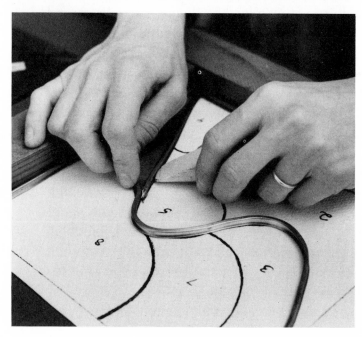
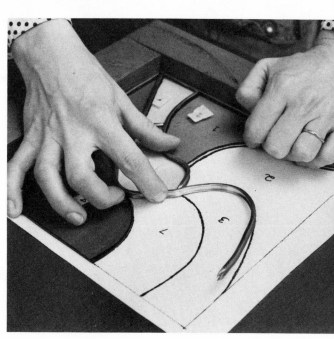

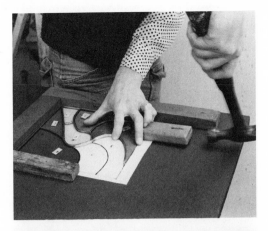

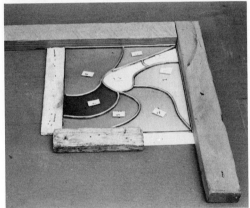

of lead for the panel were cut before assembling. You will pound some parts of the panel into place with a hammer and block of wood so that the panel will finally be one solid piece of glass that can withstand time and weathering. Lead work always sits in *tension* and must first be assembled within the frame on your table. Tension exists in the window once it is completed, and over time, the window would expand if it were not framed. Big windows must be immediately reframed after they are finished on the leading-up table. The force that holds a leaded window together comes from the outside frame, from the correct fit of the pieces of glass, from the grip of the calms, from the hardness of the putty, from the soldered joints, and in some cases even from support bars. This piece (page 25) is small and will not require a wooden frame or bars, but you should understand from the beginning the force and tension existing in a leaded piece. Possibly you can imagine why each piece must be perfectly cut. Glass is a rigid material and badly cut pieces will pop up, slip under the calm, break, or refuse to go into place in the first place, if not cut correctly. Bad cutting will cause most of your problems as you are learning. The two ways to avoid these force difficulties are to cut your pieces perfectly to begin with, and then to assemble each piece of glass *exactly* over its corresponding piece in the cartoon. Imagine how important this is when you are working on a window with nine hundred pieces of glass!

Leading up is difficult and is almost impossible to explain in a book. You will be able to grasp quickly what it means to cut or solder well. You will learn this by the process of repetition. But many of you will find yourselves running into all kinds of trouble as you begin assembling. Some of you will have to take it all apart and start all over again. This can happen to you on your first piece no matter how careful you are, but at least you'll know that what you are doing is really difficult. These beginning principles are the basis for all big windows and restoration work.

As you begin assembling, keep in mind that the goal is to make the panel one surface of level glass instead of an assemblage of unevenly stuck-together pieces of glass and lead. The cartoon is set in place in the table frame with the U-calm in place along the edges. Examine the photo sequence on leading up (pages 32–33) before you read any further, and then refer to it as you are working. Slip the corner piece (no. 1) in, so that you can see the cartoon line all around the outside edges. Here is a classic example of how you could go astray right at the beginning. If the cartoon lines do not line up on the outside edges, then either the cartoon is not exactly in place in your frame, the outside edges of U-calm lead are not perfectly in place in the corner of the table frame, or the bottom edge of the first piece is not fitted into the U-calm on the bottom side. With each piece all of these problems will come up! When you become skilled you will solve them all by feel, but for now you must intellectualize them all.

Cutting Lead

Again, the photo (page 32) shows proper hand position. You can cut your pieces as you go along or all ahead of time. For some people the tactile pleasure in working is removed if they complete a whole process at once. Be very careful not to crush the lead while cutting it. Keep your lead knife sharp by rubbing it constantly on a sharpening stone, and you will not have this problem. When a cartoon line runs into another cartoon line at an angle, cut the lead strips at the same angle. You're trying to achieve a perfect fit.

After getting the first piece of glass perfectly into position, you are ready to cut and place the first strip of H-calm lead. As in the photo, you may wish to have one or more lead strips run all the way through the design uncut, with side strips coming into the long strips. A few long lead lines are pleasing and are structurally sounder. Work the side of the H-calm firmly onto the side of the first piece by running a triangular piece of wood, called a *lathkin,* into the full length of the other side of the channel. Check the photo, because this is hard to explain. You can whittle a lathkin. The one in the photo came from my son's set of Playskool blocks.

With the H-calm cut and fitted along the outside edge of the first piece of glass, you are ready to start fitting in abutting pieces of glass. You may be tempted at this point to fit a piece most of the way in and then put a piece in behind it, figuring you can pound them both into place with a hammer against a block. This is not correct. It is true that often the fit of one piece is related to the placement of one or more pieces next to it, but you should always try to set each piece exactly in place before going on to another. Think about this concept; it is a factor in leading up that you will have to cope with. Just make sure you understand what you are doing and why you are doing it. You may find your calm slipping under glass or even glass slipping under glass. This happens because pieces are badly cut, because there are a bump or pieces of dirt under your cartoon, or because one piece of glass is much thinner than the one next to it.

Keep your table clean. If a piece of glass is extremely thin, place a piece of cardboard under it in order to bring it up to its neighbors' level. Touch the surface of your panel as you work with it. The surface should be level; you'll be in trouble sooner or later if it is not. Always raise a piece that is thin and is lower than the others. People wonder why old windows buckle over time. They buckle because the pieces weren't properly cut to begin with, or the force of the thin glass was not properly applied against the thick ones, or because the windows were not properly braced.

So you're taking it all seriously and aligning up the pieces of glass carefully, and as you add more pieces you find the middle pieces popping up. Until a middle piece is firmly in place with all the pieces around it in place, it will have a tendency to pop up. In the photos, as I hammer, notice how my fingers and palm are holding down many surrounding pieces of glass. There have been days in the studio when I have sat on a firm piece of cardboard over whole sections of a window while working on an edge or another section. This type of extreme problem only occurs while releading an old window which was improperly cut by the original glazier. He either did not allow $\frac{1}{16}$ inch between pieces of glass, or the pieces were badly cut. You will still have this problem even if you are using lead nails, which you can get from your stained glass supplier. Lead nails are flat nails to be used to hold pieces of glass in place

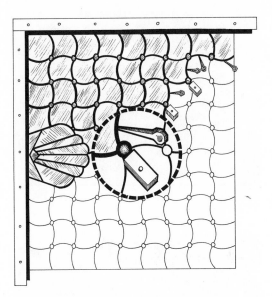

Multidirectional force and lead nails

while you're working on other sections of the window. They can be helpful, as the little illustration on the side emphasizes. But they are a deceptive force. Lead nails can make you think a piece is in right when it is getting ready to slide under another one or is pushing a neighboring piece in an odd way. Don't use them now. Learn not to rely on them right in the beginning.

Now, you have four or five pieces in position and you're pushing so hard with your fingers that they ache. You will begin to work pieces into place by hammering a block of wood against the outside edge of the piece of glass that is not fitting in. This works because the interior of the lead channel is busy molding itself to the edges of your pieces of glass. As more and bigger pieces are worked into place, only the hammer is powerful enough to force the lead channel to adhere to the glass. Pound firmly, but never hard. You should use a tapping motion. Often you will tap the block on one side many times. The greatest danger here is breakage. A piece of glass will break when it is being pounded if you hit the piece near a corner, a curve or a narrow section in the glass.

When you've worked your way over to the third side, align the edge of that side with the edge of the cartoon line and block it in with a small block of wood. You will put the U-calm on that edge later. Pound the nails through that will hold that block down before you put it on the table. Pound as few nails as possible in or near the frame, or else pieces of glass may break. When you begin putting in the third side frame you will find the force you are exerting goes now only in one direction — down. If you find at this point that the third edge does not line up exactly with the third side of your cartoon, you will have to do some more pounding or disassemble your panel. You aren't learning anything if you don't force yourself to work within the cartoon exactly. You will then work up to the top, and the rest is fairly simple. You will block in the top as you did the side. The finished leaded panel should be exactly the same size as the cartoon, with each lead line over each 1/16 inch line of the cartoon. What a sense of relief when it's all blocked and hammered in!

The description of leading up describes every possible problem you may encounter. If each piece is perfectly cut, if the 1/16 inch allowance is accurate, this panel can be assembled in one half-hour with little or no pounding and pushing. Occasionally in a class of ten students, we have one who learns effortlessly. Needless to say, we do not have to pound and push our windows, but we did in the beginning.

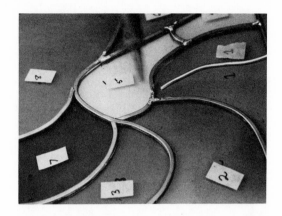

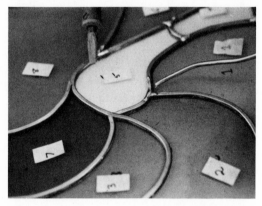

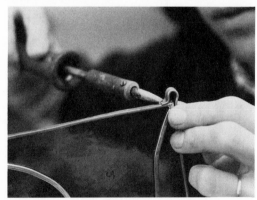

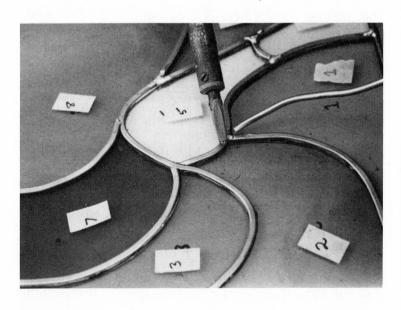

Soldering

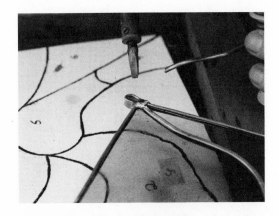

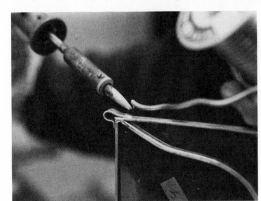

Plug in your iron and give it a few minutes to warm up. You could even practice on a few lead scraps before beginning the panel. Brush all the joints of the panel with oleic acid. You can use a small paintbrush or a rag. As you begin to solder, most of you will be afraid. If you use small amounts of solder and *never touch the joint with the iron,* you'll do very well. Use lots of oleic acid; it will keep the joint cool and help prevent it from melting if you do touch the joint with your iron. Place the solder end right over the joint and touch the end of it with your iron. Go slowly and carefully. Some of you will find it very easy. If your solder spits and splatters, your iron is too hot; unplug it for a moment. Generally you will not have this problem with the 60-watt Esico. If the solder is thick and gloppy and won't adhere, your iron is too cold. Give it a minute to get hotter. If you burn a joint slightly, add extra solder. If you really burn a hole, cut a little piece of lead calm and press it in with your lathkin. The photos show what a correctly soldered joint looks like. If some time went by between leading up and getting ready to solder, your lead joints may have oxidized slightly. Add more oleic acid.

Solder all the joints on your panel. Each joint must be totally fused and smooth when you are finished. The quality of the soldering joint is one of the means by which glaziers judge one another's work. Remove the side blocks. Place in the U lead for the sides and solder it onto the side joints. You may want to reblock it in in order to get the side joints tight. Pick up the panel.

Notice that it is already strong. Turn it over and solder all the joints on the other side. You will probably already find yourself possessing more confidence in your soldering. Most of you will want to hang this piece, so you'll want to have hooks in the top corners. Check the photo sequence to find out how to do this. A pounded piece of U-calm cut in half is being used. Form the loop before you begin soldering it on. As you solder, be really careful not to burn yourself or touch the side of the panel with your iron. When it's all soldered on, flux it and melt a little more solder all over it as in the last photo. Done!!!

A word of caution on studio chemicals and lead

Lead poisoning is a remote danger if you do a few sensible things. Don't work when you have open cuts, wash your hands frequently and rub them with lotion so they don't become chapped, and do not eat lunch on the leading up table. Lead will be on the table in flakes that apparently taste sweet. If you get acid in your eyes or on a cut, wash it out fast. Keep all acids in marked containers and know all the antidotes. Have baking soda, milk, and any other antidote around. If you burn yourself with your iron, plunge the burn into cold water to cool down the tissues. Keep plenty of Band-Aids handy.

Puttying

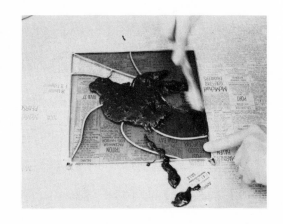

Puttying

Puttying is rubbing putty into all the calms, sealing the lead and glass. Place the panel on newspaper. Spread putty all over the panel with a brush, your fingers, or a toothbrush. Rub putty methodically into both sides of the calm, turn it over and putty the other side. Take off the excess with a brush and put it back into the putty can. Sprinkle sawdust all over one side, and rub it hard all over the panel and against the calms with your fingers, driving the putty in deep, as in the second photo of the sequence. Turn it over and do the other side. Then sprinkle whiting all over the panel and polish it with a brush. The whiting will start drying the putty and will polish the glass. Sometimes putty dries really fast, and too much will adhere to the sides of the calm. If this happens, run a pencil along the sides of all the calm. Do not breathe in any whiting — it might be wise to do this final polishing with whiting outdoors. Look at your panel. You've done it!

The procedure is the same for all lead work. I hope those of you who have this book will reread it occasionally to remind you of the simple basics of leading.

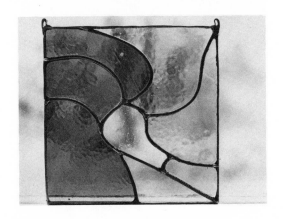

Chapter Two

Leading up a Big Window

In the first chapter the basics of lead work were covered. Complications and advanced problems were deliberately left out. The purpose of this chapter is to cover all phases of lead work so that you can also make a big window or repair an old one. And those of you who have enjoyed learning to make a small leaded piece and wish to continue making small pieces will benefit from a wider range of information on lead techniques.

Design

The first complication that develops when one wishes to make a window is design. Design is such a matter of individual preference that it is impossible to state that there is a right or wrong way to design for glass work. The problems involved are mostly in the area of choosing the most aesthetically pleasing design for each of the many different types of glass. Other problems arise when considering the future site of a window, which involves questions of architecture, and therefore only house windows will be dealt with in this book. The whole field of stained glass for churches and public buildings is vast and is being handled by large studios. The studios also have a rich history of making windows for American houses. They utilized every type of glass manufactured in Europe and America. The products of these studios can still be observed in old neighborhoods all over the country. A discussion of this long history of design may help some of you to develop your design sense and better adapt that sense for glass. Many of you may be interested in this section because you have an old window you wish to repair. You will be better equipped to restore your old window properly if you can identify the period in which it was made and therefore be knowledgeable about the materials contained in it.

The photos identify the various trends in design during different periods from 1660 to the present. The period 1660–1850 was a time when the choice of glass was a matter of utility. Glass was very expensive, and frequently it was impossible to obtain decent-sized sheets of glass. In some states people were taxed according to the sizes of their window panes, because they were an indication of affluence. The diamond-shaped windows in the photo at right were made in our studio for an exact copy of a Boston Post Road house. The original house was built in 1660. The copy was built in 1973 in Montague, Massachusetts. The windows are an absolutely authentic copy down to the last detail. Notice the thick lead, the X solder joints, the small size

"1663"

"1830" House, South Amherst, Mass.

"1865"

of the diamond lights. ("Lights" are panes of glass in a window.) The bars are wood and are pegged into the frame, and the bar ties are made of pounded lead instead of copper. These windows say a lot about American mores during Colonial times. It was considered impious to have colored glass in the home, and decoration was considered the folly of the devil. Even the old New England churches did not have stained glass. Still, one imagines that the Colonial family may have allowed themselves an occasional moment of pleasure watching the snow falling behind the lovely diamond-shaped panes of wavy blown glass. Later, there were some opaque amber, yellow, or green windows of geometrical design, particularly after 1800. It is difficult to determine whether this was because metallic impurities were hard to keep out of the glass or whether these windows were designed for privacy. You are more likely to find an opaque old window in a tavern or post house than in a private residence. The photo is an example.

Decorative consciousness began to change radically around 1850. European influences were strong, and stained glass was becoming common in American churches. People enjoyed the church windows and wished for the same beauty in their homes. This vanity was still considered by many to be the work of the devil, though, and it was a brave person who installed the first stained glass windows in his home. The photo of the 1850–1875 period window is of one made in our studio as an example of this design type. It is made of European antique glass and has many old jewels pressed by Leo Popper and Sons (New York City) in the 1880's. The church windows during this time usually showed figurative Biblical scenes or geometrical patterns made

47

of painted and fired glass. They rarely, if ever, had jewels in them. The studio designers must have attempted to make house windows as different as possible from church windows in order to avoid a clash with the virulent Puritan ethic. Domestic windows, except for those in private chapels, were never painted and fired. The later the window was made, the more likely it was to be very ornate and have many curves. The window in the photo is representative of the end of this period. Cathedral glass was rarely used in house windows, and antique and cathedral glass were not mixed. In most cases, the church windows were of painted and fired cathedral glass with some antique, and the domestic windows were of unpainted antique. Obviously, if you have such a window, it is worth repairing. Most of the glass can be matched easily. European cathedral was as cheap as American, and it can still be obtained, at a relatively high price, from New York glass importers. Windows from this period can still be found in once-fashionable neighborhoods of big cities. Pre-earthquake sections of San Francisco and the South Side of Chicago still have many lovely old houses with this style window.

Around 1875 stained glass became a fad. Exquisite windows were commissioned and installed in expensive homes, and simpler homes usually had at least one stained glass window. Many new studios were opening with fine designers working in them. These studios were usually manned by foreign laborers working sixteen hours a day cutting glass at starvation wages. Cost-cutting was never a consideration with these windows, and they show it. All types of glass were becoming common, and the barrier against mixing them was disappearing. The first examples of "art glass" were being

"1875-1895"

developed by the manufacturers. The first pieces of opal glass, satin glass, and even opalescent were experimented with. The Canadians began favoring nature scenes and Audubon reproductions, painted and fired in Europe and set in the centers of leaded windows. These windows are still common in old neighborhoods in Montreal. Still the American tendency to not paint and fire glass for house windows persisted. Some absolutely great windows were made during this period, with difficult cuts and outrageous mixtures of glass. They certainly show what can be done. The photo at left is of a pair of door-inset panes made in our studio for a carved oak door with ornate Victorian brass hinges and locks. Examples of this type of window are still fairly common in middle- and upper-class sections of cities and medium-sized small towns that were being built from 1875 to 1895.

After 1895 stained glass began to develop into an art form as well as a decorative fad. Out of the busy studios producing numerous windows, glaziers emerged who were not just fine designers but also artists. A few talented painters switched to stained glass as their medium. Louis Comfort Tiffany was one of these painters. Tiffany was also a great technician and possessed the genius to experiment with glass production techniques, which had not changed much since the Middle Ages. He opened his own glass factories on Long Island and supervised the development of Favrile and opalescent glass. Tiffany wanted texture, shading, streaking, depth, and folds in fabric to be right in the glass itself. The studios were creating figurative design, landscapes, and depth perspective by painting and firing the glass. Tiffany hated the painting and firing that limited the amount of light coming through the glass, especially when used on opalescent glass, which by its nature allows much less light to pass through than antique or cathedral does. He was also much more of an abstract artist than many people realize. He was immersed in the art nouveau obsession with plants, flowers, skies, bugs, the female form, and water, and yet he wished to create scenes of fecund nature without absolute realism. Quite a task in stained glass work.

Louis Comfort Tiffany is now receiving the admiration he deserves, but enough cannot be said about him in a book about stained glass. It is possible for one to dislike his design sense extremely and yet still learn from him about glass texture and color mixture. Tiffany Favrile glass and the work of other art nouveau glassblowers should be studied for a greater awareness of the material itself — glass.

Art nouveau windows were works of art instead of mass-produced home materials, and they were never common; from 1895 to 1915 most of the rage for glass was channeled into stained glass lamps. Almost every home had at least one. Most of your study of art nouveau windows will have to be carried on in the library. Churches in the eastern United States built during this time frequently have a window or two from Tiffany Studios, New York. The photo of the peacock is a typical re-creation of an art nouveau–style large window. The cuts are intricate. It is made of American hand-blown glass, American cathedral glass, American opalescent glass, European antique, clear glass, and many jewels. It was characteristic of art nouveau work to utilize any material, even stones, petrified wood, and shells! The

"The Peacock"

Signed Tiffany window, Unitarian Church, Amherst, Mass.

"October 1925"

window is fragile and is definitely an art piece. A window of this type is frequently foiled.

The box, "October 1925," is being used as an example of the style common from 1915 to 1925. Ornate windows were not common, and we've never been commissioned to make a window from this period, but windows that were made were strongly influenced by Tiffany's experiments. Designing in this school is rife with problems of realism in glass, of texture, and of depth in opalescent glass. Possibly it takes an artist on the scale of Tiffany to cope with the hurdles.

Today it is much harder to get unusual opalescent glass, so many young stained glass artists are making attempts to work with glassblowers in order to supervise the making of their own glass. It is easy to imagine what a decorator's delight a Tiffany window could be. Front windows overlooking congested streets could be transformed into opalescent landscapes with light filtering through into the room.

Now, windows of this type are extremely hard to find. Most of the oval insets of swans and water lilies, mountain scenes, bunches of flowers in vases have been broken over the years. They were usually small and were frequently placed up high next to the side of fireplaces or as oval insets in oak front doors. Be on the lookout for buildings of the 1920's with fireplaces, and you might spot a window on the wall next to the fireplace.

Stained glass in homes was really falling into disfavor by 1930. Mass production of consumer goods was gripping the decoration market, and money was hard to come by. The photo of "Our Home—1928" shows a window made in our studio for a Sears and Roebuck

Assemble-on-the-Site House, 1928. Sears marketed this factory-made line of houses for a few years and lost money on it.

There are few examples of windows made during this "Art Deco" period. The essence of Art Deco design is frozen motion: to freeze forever a woman's waves of hair or the leap of a gazelle, as though it would never leap again; it is a very difficult concept to work with in stained glass. The market for special windows in homes was almost nonexistent, and the studios were devoting their energies to churches in order to survive economically.

Mass production of materials for home decoration destroyed the market for decorative arts from 1940 to 1965. Occasionally, an artist or architect commissioned or designed stained glass windows, but again the idea grew in the average American's mind that stained glass windows were meant only for churches and public buildings. The studios that were founded around the turn of the century were closing, and those that were left were dealing almost exclusively with architects and church officials. They were busy developing new techniques for producing really huge windows and phasing out production of small ones. Making stained glass was beginning to be referred to as a "lost art," even though the technique is simple and the materials were still being produced.

Sometime around 1965 a "second art nouveau movement" (to coin a phrase for lack of an official title) began to surface. Suddenly the public began taking an interest in crafts people and artisans again. The artists who had become art teachers and truck drivers and practiced their craft on the side suddenly found their products in

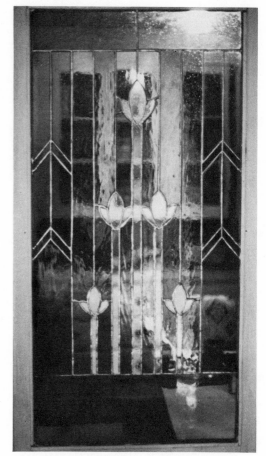

"Our Home — 1928"

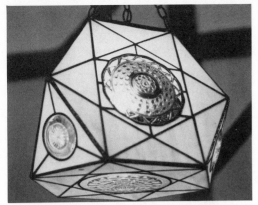

"Geometric" by Patrick Curran

"California Sagittarius" 4" square

"Winter Sunset" by Barney Zeitz

"Vines" by the Clows

demand and devoted their energies to it full time. A groundswell of younger crafts persons was working hard and becoming skilled. The photos show work done since 1970 by Patrick Curran, Barney Zeitz of Martha's Vineyard, Massachusetts and Gerry and Barbara Clow. As this book goes to press there are extremely skilled artisans all over America producing and selling great pots, blown glass, weavings, lamps, and windows. The public has again become discriminating, and the desire to treasure the things we use is important again. A huge mass-production economy of throwaways that threatened to grip our culture may not be feasible or desirable.

There is a tendency in all the arts today toward free-form design. This is a tricky concept to deal with in stained glass. Constructing a window is similar to constructing a building. Although free-form buildings are being built, each stage is carefully calculated by the architect. Free-form structure doesn't just *happen* as you work, as it can happen with a pot rising on the kick wheel or a weaving knotted by hand. If you wish to try a *free-form method* (as opposed to *free-form design*), consult the last chapter on advanced techniques in *dalles de verre.*

Lead work is exacting and requires tremendous discipline for accuracy at each stage. Your work can be only as good as or better than your first design or cartoon. You have to deal with the problem of design, of visualizing the finished work, before you cut a single piece. If you have an overwhelming desire to cut nice shapes, play with those shapes, move colors around in relation to other colors, do look up the section on *dalles de verre*.

Making a Cartoon for a Window

Begin by drawing a sketch in pencil of the design that you wish to execute. Then the sketch will have to be adapted for stained glass; pieces that are uncuttable or will break under lead stress will have to be modified. Do not execute your sketch with glass adaptation in mind—shoot for maximum creativity in your drawing and then modify it as little as possible. If you are designing for cost-cutting, then you *do* design with glass adaptation in mind. The illustrations (page 55) cover the various cutting problems. Lay out your cartoon sheet. If it is going to fit into a ready-made frame, you will have to make adjustments for the size of the frame, the rabbets, which are the grooves in a wood frame for the window edge, and the border lead. See the illustration.

You are ready to draw the cartoon on the cartoon sheet. If you are executing a copy of an old window,

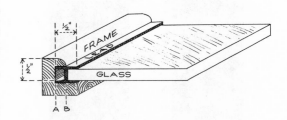

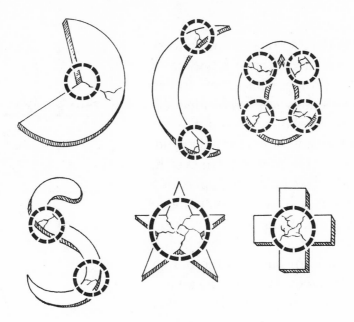

Almost uncuttable shapes

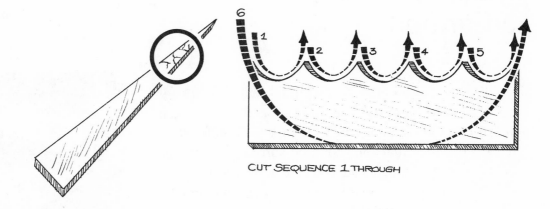

CUT SEQUENCE 1 THROUGH

Difficult cuts for foiling only

find the center, the borders, jewels, some points to work from, to adjust to scale. Be sure to have a big eraser handy. If you are working geometrically, have lots of drafting tools around. If one side is going to be identical to the other, fold the cartoon sheet down the middle and redraw the design on the other side, using the light table. If you are executing an original from your own sketch, do some really fine drawing. Make bold curves and long freehand strokes as a painter does. If you are working on a cartoon for an old window, skip to the next section on step-by-step restoration. Once you have all your pencil lines finished to your satisfaction, hang up the design and look at it from different angles. What were you trying to capture on paper? Did you succeed? Do you like it?

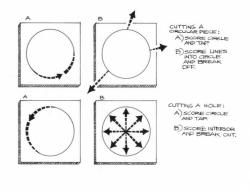

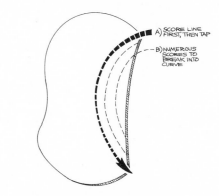

Getting a deep curve or circle

Making a Design into a Cartoon

Fill in all design lines ¹⁄₁₆ inch thick with a black felt-tip pen, then hang the cartoon up on the wall again. You'll find the dark lines are much more definite. If you have a negative reaction, don't be surprised. If there is an area of the design that you're dissatisfied with, you can glue or tape on some fresh paper over that area and redraw it. If you don't like the cartoon at all, start all over. Take your time at this stage, because everything depends on it.

Doing a cartoon to fit a frame

Selecting Glass

Now that your cartoon is finished, you will feel like you have accomplished a lot, and you'll probably feel very confident about glass selection. There are many tips on use of various types of glass in the section on history of design (pages 4–8). Observe how others have selected glass in the past. Study, think about color, keep samples of glass in your windows all over your house. This is not something that can be taught. Do select all your colors for your window before you begin cutting, because you may have to modify your cartoon for various types of glass. If you choose all opalescent, thicken all the cartoon lines slightly if the opalescent glass is thick. If you use mixtures of thick and thin glass, thicken the cartoon lines around the thick pieces. If you're using jewels, thicken the lines around them, and cut little cardboard squares to raise all the jewels slightly while leading up. Color-code your design, number all the pieces in the cartoon, and get ready to cut.

Setting up the Table for Doing the Window

Clear the table of everything. Construct a right-angle frame in one corner of 1 inch by 2 inch lumber big enough for two sides of the window. Leave a big clear space next to the window so that you can lay out all the pieces in pattern as you cut them. The photos on page 32 are filled with all sorts of setting-up tips, so study them. Cut out your pieces of glass over the cartoon at the far end of the table, or over a light table. (Instructions on building and using a light table are given at the end of the chapter.) As you cut, number each piece with stick-on labels and lay them out in formation next to the frame. When all the pieces are cut, transfer the cartoon to the frame. Go over the window pieces carefully, watching for bad cuts. Recut anything that seems to be pushing anything else out of shape.

Leading up

Cut and put in the ½ inch border lead right over the ¼ inch border of the cartoon. Begin working in the corner pieces. You may have a problem with the cartoon slipping, so for the first six inches be extra careful. If you have problems with pieces not fitting over their pieces in the cartoon, check and recheck. As you work into the window, this will give you more and more trouble. The more pieces there are in a window, the more relations, edges, thicknesses there are that can cause you to miscalculate. There are some windows that do not line up perfectly until the outside edge is hammered in. In this situation, you must have faith. Those pieces are cut the same size as those pieces in that cartoon. There is room for that lead to be there. With enough hammering and pushing, that window will go together. However, there are so many variables that your window will not be exact. You can produce a "perfect" window if you are willing to spend four times the normal time on it. If that is your goal, do it.

Once you are rolling along, your experience, or lack of experience, will take over. You'll encounter situations, somewhat like each bridge hand, that are new, and will make you reexamine any problems you've had to solve in leading up before. You will have to solve all of them by yourself. You have all this glass and lead in your hands, you push at it and pound it; pressures are flying in all directions. You are at liberty, you are the boss, you must decide what must be done. If you're tired, quit for a while or you will break a piece. You are going to encounter all kinds of situations that cannot be covered in a book, and you'll just have to keep in mind the fragile nature of glass, the idea of pressures and buckles, the malleability of lead.

There are four major problems.

Blocking in

You are dealing with a larger area, you may decide you need to use lead nails. Keep the pressure working down to the corner until you block in the side.

Buckling

When pressures are too many or too much, particularly when you have little pieces back to back as in the Peacock's tail, you may have to solder sections as you go to prevent buckling. You will avoid having to solder oxidized joints that you'd have to sand later, but if you have made a mistake, it is doubly hard to correct it.

Cutting yourself

Be careful, particularly when you're working with the lathkin. Keep Band-Aids around and quit when you're tired.

Being accurate

Inevitably pieces will wander because of lead, unseen pressures, slightly inaccurate cutting. Sometimes it is just impossible to find the source of the problem or too difficult to correct it. You can make compensations with later pieces. Sometimes it is wise to cut down or enlarge an edge, a top or corner piece. Keep in touch with your window, touch it to see if it is solid, if it is warping, if it feels good. Be confident; soon it will be finished and it will be magnificent.

Some Problems in Leading up a Big Window

The various special problems that you will encounter while doing any ambitious lead work are discussed at the end of this chapter.

Complete Restoration of an Old Window

First of all, you will need a cartoon. Some glaziers take the old window apart piece by piece, re-lead it, and solder it as they work along. This is very time-consuming and will not work on a big window such as the one on page 63 because you will not know you are off until you get to the other side. This window dates back to circa 1895, and it is exquisite; the owners were amazed at its beauty after we finished.

Before you begin the cartoon, remember to photograph the old window for reference. You will do the cartoon in stages. The first stage is to do all sorts of measuring and marking on the cartoon sheet from the old window for reference points. For example, if there is a bottom border in the window that is 6½ inches wide, draw in a line on the cartoon sheet that corresponds to that border. If there is a jewel in the window centered 13½ inches from each side, 16 inches from the top, and 36 inches from the bottom, mark a center point for that jewel. Remember, you will not be able to take any of these measurements once you've disassembled the window! The second stage of the cartoon is to draw around the key pieces you've measured after you've disassembled them. Mark that central jewel or center flower you've drawn around as a "key piece," and every time you work your way toward that piece while re-leading,

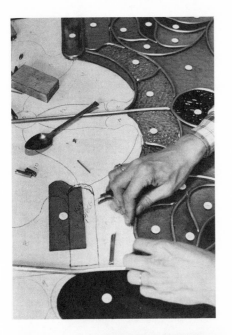

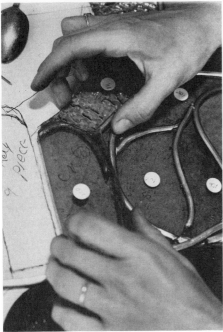

check to make sure the piece fits over it exactly. The third stage in completing the cartoon is drawing around *each* piece of glass in place after you have removed it and washed it. This is not necessary, but it can keep you out of trouble, and you will have a complete cartoon of the old window.

One of the difficulties with restoration is that it can be boring. If you do it in stages and throw out the old assembly-line concept, it is easier to cope with. Put the cartoon sheet in the frame. In order to take apart the old window, lay it flat on the other end of your table. Pull a bottom or corner section off the edge of the table, melt the joints on both sides with a soldering iron, and work out the pieces with the grozers. Melt the joints until the piece is ready to slip out. Some pieces you will be able to remove by just pulling on them. Do not put undue stress on any of the old pieces; go slowly, and never twist the pieces from side to side. Take apart a whole section up to a key piece, then remove that key piece and draw around it according to your measurements. Soak all the pieces in household ammonia and water, but do not soak painted and fired pieces! Wash them carefully by hand. They will need to soak quite a while, so you might want to have two ammonia baths — put all the pieces from the second section in the second bath, take apart a third section, and then remove all the pieces of the first batch from the bath, and scrub them with steel wool. Do not mix batches! When you have a batch cleaned and dried, lay it out in place on the cartoon and draw around the pieces, then lay out the pieces in place next to the cartoon sheet. All the pieces will gradually line up for the re-lead job.

Possible Dangers with Old Windows

Again, never soak painted and fired pieces in ammonia. Wash them in warm soapy water. Never steel-wool them or you will scrape the paint off. Watch out for crackle glass: don't rub your fingers over its surface. When you're ready to putty it, put masking tape all over it. Otherwise, putty will get into the surface and will not come out. Don't throw away broken pieces; if you cannot match an old piece, you may wish to copper foil or lead a break. Be especially careful of early opalescents in windows made in the 1880's and 1890's: you can't match them, and you may decide to glue breaks in rare glass with glass glue.

After the pieces have soaked long enough, rub them all over with steel wool. You'll be absolutely delighted to see the glass come alive. When you are releading, you can solder section by section. Be careful when you hammer old glass; it is really fragile. Putty the window as you would a new one.

The last section of this chapter is an index of specific problems and special tools and materials. It is meant to be used as reference as you are first learning to do lead work. Many of you will never see some of these problems. Putty formula is included here rather than earlier in the book because many of you will always buy your putty and never need to make your own. Framing and bracing problems are here for the same reason—many of you will have a carpenter solve these problems for you.

More Complicated Tools and Supplies

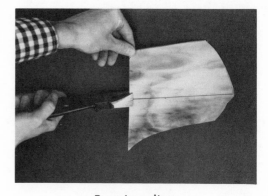

Running pliers

Running pliers

See the photo at right. You may find these at your stained glass supplier's store. Ask him how to use them. You should line up the line on the head with the score mark. Tighten the pliers until the outside corners grip the glass. Grip the handle slightly, loosen the screw slightly, and crack! the score line will run. This is an invaluable tool for breaking small to medium cuts in opalescent glass only. This tool eliminates tapping, which is especially undesirable with opalescents because it causes so many bumps.

Diamond cutter

It will save you hours of time cutting clear glass, and the results with anything else are pretty poor. If you buy one, don't let anyone else use it—the diamond is likely to pop out.

Selenium steel cutter

Ask your supplier for one. They are terrific and inexpensive, and will solve all cutting difficulties with red, yellow, or amber glass.

Opalescent steel cutter

Also terrific.

Putty

Mix equal parts of portland cement, whiting, and plaster of paris. Mix linseed oil into the mixture until it is peanut butter consistency. Don't make more than you can use immediately.

Some Techniques

Puttying for weatherseal

For an indoor-outdoor leaded window, particularly one that will have high wind and rain stress, you must be especially careful to get putty in all the calms. Putty the window top to bottom, the direction in which the water will run.

How to make a light table

The ideal is to sink a ½-inch-thick piece of glass about 1 foot by 2 feet into your stained glass table top, another table top, or a 1-inch-thick piece of plywood, which can be used for a table top. Acid-etched frosted glass is the best because it will cut down on glare. You can have a carpenter do this for you with a router. A box can be constructed underneath the glass and lined with foil, or you can reflect natural light under it with an angle mirror, or you can just put a light fixture underneath it.

Construction of a stained glass table

Sturdiness and size are what is important. Find the largest 1-inch-thick piece of plywood you can. Five by ten feet is ideal, since you may assemble a really big window someday. Buy a big old table if you can. If you construct one, make the legs and bottom crosspieces out of 2 by 4's and 4 by 4's. Assemble it with big bolts in case you want to take it apart again. Do not plan to store glass under your table.

Construction of glass bins

Frame the bins out of 2 by 4's and ½-inch plywood. They should be 4 feet high in case you start getting glass from the factories. Frame in a divider every 8 inches. You will not want to put in more than ten sheets in a section or you'll have breakage.

Bracing a window

Bracing a window means installing metal bars in the wood frame and soldering wires on the lead joints of the window to twist around the bars. You will need iron bars, which are hard to get, though most metal shops carry some sizes. There are many ways to install them in the frame, but they should be installed permanently. The window can be removed by opening the wires, but the bars will stay in place. Generally, the bars should be on the outside. See the illustration for where to brace.

Framing a window

A stained glass window frame has to have a rabbet wide and deep enough for lead. If you are going to hold the lead in with quarter round molding, the rabbet will also have to be deep enough for the molding. Generally the width of the rabbet should be ⅜ inch so that a little bit of the ½-inch border lead shows.

Special Cutting Problems

Thick edges

Cut off all the thick sections of the sheet and save them for foiling later. Never try to lead them up.

Flashed glass

Flashed glass is clear glass with a thin layer of color adhering to it or stained glass with a layer of color over it, such as red over light blue (made in Germany). It is made for etching, which is the removal of the color layer to reveal the glass underneath. Etching techniques are covered in Chapter Five. Flashed glass is also used for its intense color. Cut flashed glass on the unflashed side. Look at the edge of the glass and you can usually see the clear glass and the flash on one side. Mark the flashed side with chalk. If you can't see which side is flashed, you can chip away one of the edges. The flash will tend to chip off more than the clear glass. Try not to groze pieces of flashed glass that you have cut, since the color will chip off on the edges and it will show after you've leaded the pieces up.

Selenium glass

Yellows, ambers, and reds are made with selenium. They are very hard to cut. Get a selenium cutter if you plan to use many of these colors.

Badly tempered glass

Glass that will not break on its score line, that cracks as you are scoring it, or that makes a dull thudding sound when you tap it hard with your finger is badly tempered. The manufacturer has not annealed it prop-

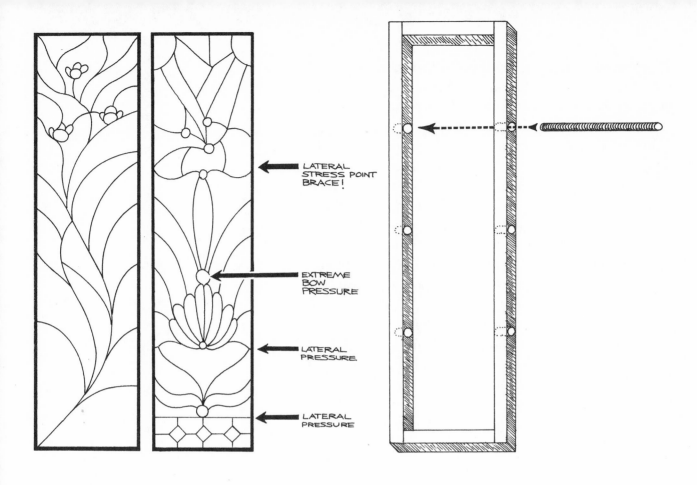

LATERAL
STRESS POINT
BRACE!

EXTREME
BOW
PRESSURE

LATERAL
PRESSURE.

LATERAL
PRESSURE

Bracing a window

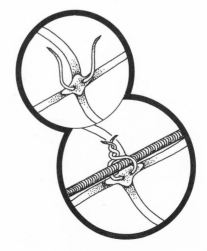

erly. (Annealing is cooling the sheets of glass after they have been made in the kiln.) When you are buying glass, try to avoid sheets with wildly varying thicknesses. More often than not, they are badly tempered, and they won't fit into lead calms, anyway. If you get some badly tempered glass, about all you can do is try to cut it in the direction it is inclined to break. Use it for easy cuts or big pieces, or put it aside for lamp templates. Watch out for it, because it can be very dangerous. When you are tapping it, it has a tendency to break unexpectedly, fall and cut your foot. It is best to use only straight cuts on it and to snap the cuts off the edge of the table swiftly. Also watch out for *sheets that shatter*. Generally this happens only with antique glass that has been in storage for seventy years or so and has become brittle like old crystal. Be careful. Often you can restore the suppleness of the tone by cutting the sheet into quarters; you'll find the quarter pieces seem to be strong. As mentioned before, the bigger a piece of glass is, the more unstable it is.

Cutting big sheets

Really big surfaces of glass are rarely useful except in the big studios. For safety and storage, it is wise to cut big sheets down when they arrive. Some of you may send for a crate of glass that has 4-foot by 10-foot sheets. Your aim is to get a perfectly straight edge. Lay out the sheet on an absolutely flat table or floor. Using a ruler, score the glass in a straight line in one, two, or three places, depending upon the size you want. Slowly and carefully slide a piece of ½-inch by 1-inch wood trim under the score line. Line up the piece of trim so that it is *exactly* under one side of the score line. Apply even pressure downward on the other side with a piece of 2 by 4 or with another person. You will get a nice clean break. Running pliers are reputed to be good for straight cuts in big sheets.

Bubbles, warps, color defects, surface ridges

These are often a blessing in disguise. Save them until you are skilled; they can be the focal point of a window.

Clean edges

For some copper foil work, and some leadwork with small pieces and extremely thin lead, clean edges may be necessary. Breaking pieces with the running pliers, snapping off pieces between fingers, or snapping off cuts on the table edge will prevent most bumps on edges. Grozing or using a file will take bumps off. A grinding wheel will take anything off. Many glaziers have a grinding wheel with water running on it set up right next to their table. Always wear safety glasses when working on the grinding wheel.

Many more pages could be written on lead techniques and restoration work. The emphasis in the whole chapter has been learning from the past. In some ways the best way to learn how to handle the leading up of complicated windows would be to work on old windows. As a beginner, you will encounter great difficulties getting the glass you want. An old window, however, usually has many different types of glass and will teach you about possible and impossible cuts in glass. Old windows with 90 percent of the pieces intact are still readily available for very little money. A leaded window is practically worthless on the antique market if even one piece is broken. Completely restored, it is often worth hundreds of dollars. Consider buying an old window, following the steps on restoration, and then attempting your first window from start to finish.

Chapter Three

Copper Foiling

The second basic stained glass technique to be mastered is copper foiling. This was the method preferred by Louis Comfort Tiffany, and copper foiling is also referred to as "the Tiffany technique." Thin strips of copper are wrapped around each piece of glass, the copper joints are *tacked* together with dabs of solder, then all the copper seams are *floated* with solder. Solder is 60 percent tin and 40 percent lead, so it resembles lead calm somewhat when it is *floated* into a straight seam. Copper foiling fell into disuse until very recently, and many people still think that foiled shades are leaded. However, copper foiling is again a popular technique, and new materials such as adhesive foil have been developed to make it easier.

You will need a roll of ½-inch and a roll of ³⁄₁₆-inch adhesive copper foil, a can of Nokorode soldering paste, and a good pair of scissors to get started. While you are getting the materials at your stained glass suppliers, pick up a 6-inch side roll of nonadhesive foil and a bag of copper sulfate crystals.

The Fish and alternative designs

The first project is an intricate hanging piece, "The Fish." It is especially designed to teach all the possibilities in foiling, and it is difficult. If your goal is simply to make ornaments out of a few pieces of glass, then make your own design or use one of the optional designs. If you make the fish, you will really know how to foil when you are finished and you will be ready to go right into lamps. Anybody can make the fish, but it will take a long time. Go slowly and methodically. If you make your own design, notice that in foiling, the lines between the pieces of glass are not blacked in 1/16 inch thick. The foiling cartoon has normal design lines because allowance does not have to be made for lead calm.

The cutting will take a surprisingly long time. Use clear or light glass if you do not have a light table. Now you will really see why pattern cutting is not advised. The fish cannot possibly be cut with patterns. When cutting the tiny pieces, do not press too hard, or you will shatter the glass. Place the pieces in formation next to your cutting area and see how they are lining up. For the hardest pieces, attempt to select thin glass; thick glass is harder to cut and harder to foil. If you use colored glass, notice the tremendous variations in glass thickness as you put the fish together. If you are using all clear glass, you won't notice these variations. You will find the varying thicknesses hard to foil, but learning to work with varying thicknesses of glass is part of learning to foil. The fish will catch the light, and the light will play on the uneven surface, producing a delightful effect.

When the pieces are all cut, you're ready to foil. Precut rolls of adhesive foil, or nonadhesive foil that you must cut, can be used. The adhesive foil is more expensive but is a great labor-saver. Around the turn of the century, strips of copper were cut and adhesive was brushed onto the copper strips. Wrapping pieces of glass is difficult, and the adhesive makes the job much faster. The widths of the adhesive foil are not correct for all thicknesses of glass, and you will still often need to cut the width of the rolls down before you strip off the backing. A roll of ¼-inch and a roll of ³⁄₁₆-inch adhesive foil will be adequate for most thicknesses of glass.

To begin foiling, check the thicknesses of your glass against the two widths of your foil. When you hold the foil against the edge of the glass, a tiny edge of foil should be visible which will overlap onto the surface of the glass. Three-sixteenths foil will be ideal for most glass. Cutting the ¼-inch foil in half and using both sides of it will be ideal for thinner edges of glass. For the thinnest pieces of antique glass, cutting ³⁄₁₆-inch foil in half may be ideal. Widen the foil if a thick line is a part of your design. If this seems absurdly exacting, remember that foiling is a jeweler's art; it is a bit like cloisonné. This exercise really teaches you what foiling is rather than producing an object that can be marketed. The fish would have to be very expensive!

When you have worked out foil thickness problems, you are ready to wrap each piece with foil. As you work, keep reforming the fish. Take your first piece of glass in hand as in the photo and train yourself to be conscious of front and back sides of the glass. It will become instinctive. You can train yourself to know front and back sides by the surface quality of the glass, by an awareness of how each piece fits into the pattern, or by always

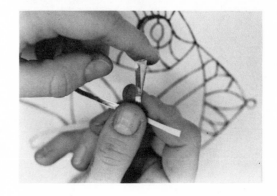

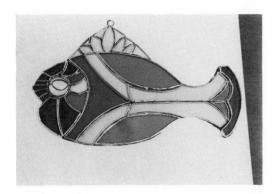

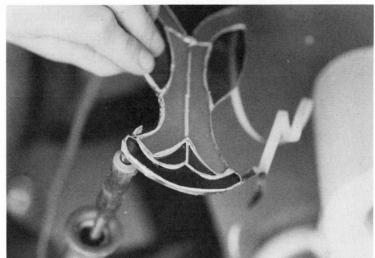

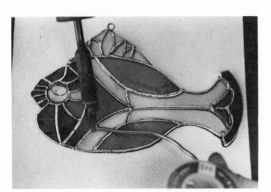

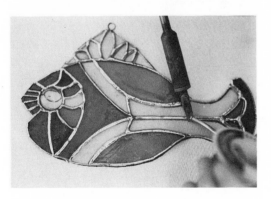

pressing the front side with a certain finger as you work. If you use the finger placement method, you can almost shut your eyes while you work. Hold the piece of glass almost right in front of your nose and train your eye on the front surface. Take the foil of proper width, peel off enough adhesive for one side, place the sticky section up against the edge, and line it up so that a tiny edge of the foil is visible on the edge of the front side. Press the sticky side to the side of the glass. Do not think about the underside of the glass because if the foil is the proper width, the underside will always be perfect provided the front side is lined up properly. Press the tiny overlap onto the front surface of the glass. You can make it stick firmly by running a fingernail or a wooden implement along it. Chopsticks, for example, can be very handy while foiling.

On the second side the same procedure is followed. The corner is turned and the corner is folded over and tucked under like the corner of the sheet while making a bed. Finish the other sides and put the piece back in place in the fish. Do all the pieces, varying the thickness of the foil according to the thickness of the glass in each piece.

You are ready to *tack* together all the pieces. Transfer the fish to the cartoon as in the photo. When larger pieces are foiled, each one is *tinned* for extra strength. That is, each piece is rubbed with flux after it is foiled, and solder is floated on the pieces before they are tacked together. In this case, the pieces in the fish are too small and this step is eliminated. In *tacking,* dab some soldering paste on each joint or place it in the fish where pieces fit together at the corners. You will have a lot of trouble with little pieces sticking to your fingers as you flux joints. When you have flux on the joints, dab solder on or *tack* the joints so that the fish is held together.

The fish is *floated* after it is tacked together. Rub all the seams and joints with soldering paste. Set the fish up so that it is absolutely level — the key to floating is to have the seams level. Hold the end of the solder close to the seam and melt it off, moving along the seam with the soldering iron. The iron can't melt the copper, so you do not have to worry about touching the seam with the iron. The object is to form a nice rounded seam that covers all of the copper. When the fish is all floated, including the outside edge, wrap the outside of the fish with ¼-inch foil. With your iron, apply the second layer of foil, then coat the new layer of foil very liberally with soldering paste. Float this, so that all the joints that come into the edge of the fish are a part of the outside edge. This is hard and will take some time. Finish the fish by soldering on a brass ring or a rolled piece of copper foil so that it can be hung.

Clean the fish by scrubbing it all over with a toothbrush and straight ammonia. Polish it with a soft rag. You can consider the fish finished if you like the shiny silvery seams. You can turn the seams a coppery color by scrubbing them with copper sulfate crystals in ammonia. Use about ½ cup ammonia and enough crystals to turn the solution a bright blue green. The seams can be turned to a pewter finish by rubbing them with a mixture of copper sulfate crystals and tinner's fluid. Tinner's fluid can be obtained at any hardware store. After you have obtained the desired finish, scrub the fish with ammonia on a toothbrush until it is sparkling clean. You have finished your first copper foil project.

Copper foiling is an excellent craft for relaxation after

work. Foiling can be done in a small space, it is time-consuming and the intricacy is highly satisfying. Foiling is a small-muscle craft and affords the same type of pleasure as knitting or making jewelry. As you have probably discovered by now, it can be very difficult to get glass, particularly a variety of glass. Small scraps can be used for foiling, and studios often sell small scraps by the pound. Besides getting pure pleasure from foiling, you can make extremely salable objects. The second project is a copper foil box, which would be very marketable, and the third project is a small copper foil lamp, also very salable.

The pattern for the top of the box is, again, difficult and will teach you a lot about foiling. You can make any design for the box top as long as it is the same size as the top in "October 1925." You will need a piece of mirror glass from your hardware store or glass supplier, for the bottom, a pair of small hinges of thin brass from your hardware store, and a small piece of felt from your lamp repair store or fabric supplier. Making the box will require some new skills; you will learn how to construct with glass, which will finally lead up to lamp making.

Cut all the pieces. The top of the box will take the longest unless you are making it of one piece of glass. If you make up the design in the book, attach and float an extra piece of copper foil around the edge of the top. That is the top rim of the box, and it must be strong. With any box-top design, extra foil must be added to the back of the top, where you will attach the hinges. Foil all the pieces with the rolled adhesive foil that is closest to the proper width. Do not cut foil for large pieces. The edges of the foil must be absolutely uniform. Tin the side and bottom pieces. Tinning means to flux and float the big

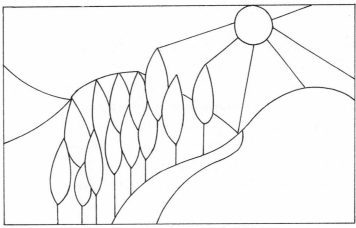

B) TOP AND BOTTOM OF BOX CUT TO SAME SIZE

"October 1925"

HINGE ALLOWANCE

CUT TWICE FOR SIDES

BOX BACK, CUT ON DOTTED LINE __

BOX FRONT FULL SIZE ___

pieces before assembling the box. As with the fish, you do not tin the pieces in the intricate top.

The box pieces are ready to be assembled. The important concept to keep in mind when making boxes is that all *interior edges must be contiguous* so there is a resulting 90-degree outside seam that can be floated with a perfect seam of solder. The illustration will aid in understanding this. Set the bottom piece on the table. Place the best side downward so that it will be the visible bottom, unless you are going to felt the bottom. If you are going to felt the bottom (usually advisable, because the box might otherwise scratch a good table), have the best side of the glass or the mirror front facing up. Place one of the 3-inch-by-5-inch pieces at a 90-degree angle to the bottom with the inside edges contiguous. You can hold it up against a carpenter's square or a right-angle box to get an accurate angle. Run the soldering iron along the inside of the bottom edges in order to fuse the two inside contiguous pieces. Take one of the 3-inch-by-3-inch sides and place it at a 90-degree angle to the bottom inside edge and to the inside edge of the 3 by 5 piece. Fuse both those sides. Construct the other two sides. The box bottom is tacked together. The shorter 3 by 5 (actually 2⅞ inches by 5 inches) is the box back. Strengthen the top of the box back with extra strips of foil, as was done with the box top. The hinges will pull slightly, and those two edges must be extra rigid. It is advisable to make those two edges even a little wider, using wider foil.

Float the box bottom completely before attaching the top. Coat all the seams with flux. Use lots of solder when floating and keep the seams level by propping the box up when necessary. Do a neat job of floating the

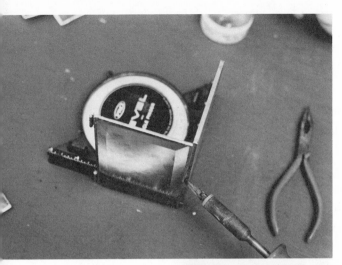

Making the box

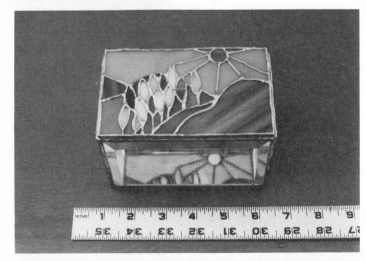

interior. Clean the box bottom thoroughly, wiping it first with paper towels and then washing it out with ammonia.

Hinges can also be purchased at the hobby store. Small decorative hinges of shiny brass, which are marketed for the hobbyist making wooden boxes, are the best. Buy the ones made of thin brass, because you will have to cut off the section that is supposed to be attached to the sides of a wooden box. Handmade hinges can be made by cutting and looping $1/64$ inch thick brass or copper over brass pins. This is very difficult and requires hours of maddening fussing and burning of fingers. If you want to make your own hinges, buy a pair of commercial ones and examine them to understand the principle involved.

You have your pair of hinges in hand. Attach them to the side of the box first, since this seems to be easier. Cut off enough of the hinges so that you can solder them to the box without having part of the hinge protrude onto the glass surface. See the illustration, page 00. Two dangers of working with hinges are burning yourself and getting solder into the workings of the hinge. Hold the hinge with pliers, preferably jewelry pliers, which can also be used to cut the hinges; and use solder and flux very sparingly. Solder is very strong, so you don't need much of it to secure them.

You are ready to attach the top. If you wish to antique the box with copper sulfate crystals, do it before attaching the top. If you chose to use a mirror for your box bottom, consider not antiquing the box. The shiny solder looks very chic with the mirror surface. Line up the box top. The back of the box is slightly shorter to allow for the extra height caused by the attachment of the hinges.

Solder the hinges to the back of the boxtop. Smooth out the solder or antique it if you did the rest of the box. The last step is to felt the bottom. Cut a piece of felt — green is traditional — to match the bottom. Spread Elmer's Glue on the felt, stick it to the bottom and press it on with a book, and let it dry. Do not spread glue on the mirror backing as it might show on the other side. You are finished.

The last copper foil project is a lantern. This lantern can be very simple, made of as few as eight pieces of glass, or it can be very complex, but making it does not require any new skills. When you complete it, it can be wired at a hardware or lamp store.

Lanterns can be foiled or leaded. This one (page 90) a type popular in England around 1800, could be lovely as a greeting piece on the front porch. If it is to be used outside, it must be leaded. It would not be advisable to place it where it can get wet because of the wiring. Instructions are given here only for foiling it. If you want to lead it, assemble each side and putty each side as you would do four little windows. Right-angle lead is available at the stained glass suppliers for the four corners. Assemble the four top pieces, bending them slowly for the top angles. Be sure to putty the top too!

The intricacy of the design in the illustration is very representative of the type of candle-lit lantern that might have been found in a popular roadhouse. The English examples were assembled in decorative polished brass frames and the panels were usually foiled or wrapped in thin brass stripping.

The pattern in the illustration (page 92) will have to be doubled. The finished lamp in the photos is 6 inches by 9 inches, which was the size of the nineteenth-century

English type. The type of glass and the way it is used is also representative of the English style. The glass is European antique, the center is amethyst, row 2 is emerald green, row 3 is dark amber, and rows 4 and 5 are light amber. The border is of opalescent and is not particularly representative. The border in this modern lantern is a somewhat satisfactory substitute for the polished

Making the lantern

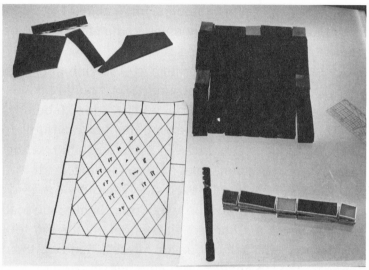

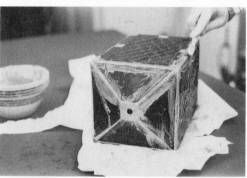

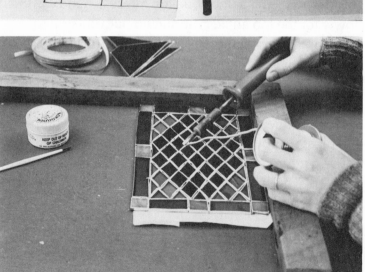

filigreed brass the original would have had. The extra squares of sky-blue opalescent are very decorative.

Cut, foil, and assemble the four lantern sides. Be very careful to make them exactly the same size as the 6 by 9 inches indicated because the body of the lamp must be exactly square, or the top will not fit. Antique the four sides before doing the top. The finish on the lamp in the photos is a *very* deep coppery color, which is characteristic of antiquity. Extra copper sulfate crystals and hard rubbing with a toothbrush will turn the foil a deep copper color. Foil and tin the four top pieces. Do not antique them until the lantern is assembled; antiqued joints do not fuse well.

Assemble the four box sides before you attach the top. For accuracy draw a perfect 6-inch square. Line up the sides over the 6-inch square, and you will have perfect right-angle corners. When you fuse the side seams, the copper sulfate finish will give you trouble. Melt the solder on the sides, fuse the sides, flux the seams, float them neatly, and you will re-antique the side seams when you antique the top. The top would seem to present a problem, but it is really very simple. Take two top pieces in hand; on the drawing of the 6-inch square, line up the bottom edges of the two pieces, which will be fused to the tops of the sides. Draw together the angular seam that will run from the joint of the box sides to the top of the lantern and fuse it with the soldering iron. Half of the top is now ready to be fused to the body of the lantern. Line up the half with the body of the box and fuse the seam at the top. Attach the other two parts of the top. Flux all the seams and float them. Antique the shiny soldered areas to match the body of the lantern, and you are finished.

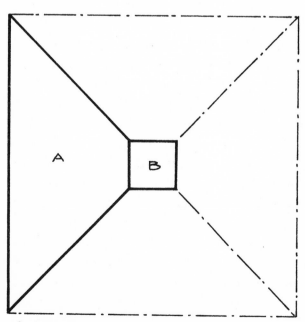

O.	BSB.	O.	BSB.	O.

(Grid of diamond panels)

LT. A. LT. A. DK. A. LT. A. LT. A.
LT. A. LT. A. DK. A. DK. A. LT. A. LT. A.
LT. A. DK. A. G. DK. A. LT. A.
LT. A. DK. A. G. G. DK. A. LT. A.
DK. A. G. A. G. DK. A.
DK. A. G. A. A. G. DK. A.
DK. A. G. A. G. DK. A.
LT. A. DK. A. G. G. DK. A. LT. A.
LT. A. DK. A. G. DK. A. LT. A.
LT. A. LT. A. DK. A. DK. A. LT. A. LT. A.
LT. A. LT. A. DK. A. LT. A. LT. A.

BSB. (left)				BSB. (right)
O. (left)				O. (right)
BSB. (left)				BSB. (right)

| O. | BSB. | O. | BSB. | O. |

COLOR CODE: P-PURPLE, G-GREEN, DK.A-DARK AMBER
LT. A-LIGHT AMBER, BSB-BROMO SELTZER
BLUE, O-OPAL.

The lantern pattern

A) CUT TOP FOUR
TIMES AND REPEAT
AROUND 1" SQ. COPPER TOP (B)

Wiring lamps will scare many of you. Wiring is actually not that difficult, but lamp parts, especially, for stained glass can be a big problem. Special support bars, vase caps, and lamp hardware are hard to come by. Other books pass this problem off and advise you to buy commercial *vasecaps* and suggest the usage of *fixture straps* or "crossbars." The top cap, or vasecap, is merely decorative, and it is all right to use one. The brass vasecaps can be fluxed and floated so that they match the copper foil. The thorny problem with lamps is finding solutions for supporting the weight of the glass. All sorts of special hardware was being manufactured just for stained glass shades sixty years ago and the lampmaker did not have to worry about this problem.

A 1-inch square of 1/32-inch copper was used on the lantern in the photos. First it was soldered securely into the four corner joints, then it was soldered onto the foil on the lamp top, then solder was floated all over the square, and the top was antiqued to match the finish of the lantern. This is an absolutely secure support for this lantern, and 1/16-inch to 1/32-inch copper, cut to size with holes drilled for the wiring parts, is reliable and secure support for the heaviest copper foil shade that can be made. The advantages of using sheet copper cut to size are threefold: the copper solders permanently to the joints of the lamp, the copper antiques easily, and the cut piece can be soldered to all the joints in the lamp even if the lamp has 36 templates. The joints are what give a heavy shade strength. Crossbars do not solder securely to copper because they are made of aluminum—in addition, they have only two ends and therefore cannot adhere to all the joints meeting in the top surface. In order to solve the supply problem for this lantern and for future lamps, find someone who can cut copper sheeting to size for you or learn to do it yourself. We have a tinsmith who does this for our lamps. Also be sure to collect old parts that were designed for stained glass shades. Often lamp bases have harps with strong rings at the top designed for the weight of shades. Buy them if you see them.

For the lantern body you will need a 1-inch square of copper, or brass will do. Your lamp store expert may be able to help you on this one. Solder the square securely to the top of the lantern, float it, and antique it. For wiring, follow the instructions in the illustration at right on wiring the lantern. As mentioned before, you can have this done at a lamp store. Your lamp parts will cost you so much, that sometimes it is almost as cheap to have the lamp store expert wire it. You will have to cope with the support top in most cases. A 25- or 40-watt candlelight-type bulb is best in this lantern. Enjoy.

The crucial question is whether to lead or foil. Many of the books on the market on lamps are filled with leaded lamp projects. We see what leaded shades look like after a few years of use, because people bring them to us for repair. We will not even repair them unless they are shades that were specially designed for lead, such as the shade in the photo at left. Pat's leaded shade is the proper weight for leading, with just a few large pieces in the shade. The shade has a large area for the electric light bulb. The seams are decorated with twisted lead, which lends extra strength and complements the Moorish quality of this shade. Lead is not a good interior metal, with exceptions. Lead can be strik-

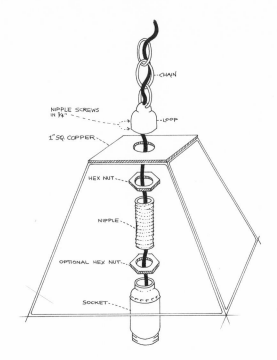

Wiring instructions for lantern

Opalescent leaded lampshade by Patrick Curran

ing in a Spanish or Moorish decor, a very simple Early American kitchen, or in a handmade house that emphasizes clay, wood, and metal surfaces. Copper foil, properly finished, is appropriate with the most elegant fabrics, glasswares, and precious metals of a formal interior.

High standards of quality are being established as artisans who work with the various media of glass are becoming more skilled. Lamps should be foiled except for special cases, and windows should be leaded except for special cases. Windows can be foiled if they are too intricate to lead. Tiffany loved to foil huge windows. But foiled windows cannot be exposed to weather because they are too rigid to withstand wind pressure, and because water (and ice!) will seep through the seams. Tiffany installed his foiled art windows between interior rooms and in covered porches or verandas, or he had them installed in special double frames with protective clear glass on the outside. Frequently he would foil only certain sections of his windows and lead a protective layer of clear glass behind the foiled section.

You must be sure that the proud owner of one of your foiled art pieces realizes that glass must be set behind the piece if it is to be used as a window. Also, interior pieces such as firescreens and interior decorative screens must be foiled in most cases. Lead simply is not a proper interior material, with a few exceptions.

The labor factor is also important when deciding to lead or foil. Initially, leading may seem much easier to most of you. But as you become more skilled at foiling, you will start working very fast and you will notice how much lead limits possible complexity in windows. Do think about foiling windows as you become more skilled.

Chapter Four

Lamps

Glass is such an inherently beautiful material that it is difficult to make it into an ugly object. It is hard to understand why so many intricately crafted lamps ended up gathering dust in the attic or being destroyed at the dump. Fashion changes, interior design evolves, objects fall into disfavor because they do not fill a need or were poorly made to stand the test of time. Opalescent lampshades, now popularly known as "Tiffany shades," were developed seventy years ago for the aesthetic utilization of electric lighting. Before the invention of electricity, gaslight was used to light the interior; and before gaslight, oil lamps, candles, and firelight were used. Within shell-like blown glass shades, gaslight was just as lovely as candles, firelight, and oil lamps had been in their time. But electric lights, obviously extremely practical, must have seemed garish to our turn-of-the-century ancestors. Today, the need to soften electric light is even more of a problem in modern decor because wattages have risen tenfold since the inception of electric lighting. Therefore, the reason opalescent lamps and shades fell into disfavor surely cannot be because they were no longer useful. Their total disappearance from American home interiors must be attributed to the general flow of art history (discussed earlier in Chapter Two on window design). Beautifully crafted objects were overwhelmed in the flood of mass-produced goods for the home.

Windows, leaded or foiled, have never been mass-produced and probably never will be. But lamps have been mass-produced before and are being mass-produced at the present time. Judging by the quality of many present-day mass-produced stained glass shades, it is possible to imagine that the quality of the turn-of-the-century shades may have contributed to their demise. Many modern inexpensive mass-produced shades are leaded instead of foiled, and they are often made of unoriginal square cuts of cathedral glass. Cathedral glass does not soften light as opalescent glass does, but the more important fact is that these lamps will fall apart within a few years because lead sags with weight over time. At the studio, people frequently bring us twisted and oxidized preformed pattern lamps made sixty years ago of poured pot metal. These lamps obviously were too heavy and badly balanced, and they were made of big panels of opalescent glass that quickly cracked and broke. A properly constructed copper foil shade is extremely strong. The real Tiffany shades from Tiffany Studios, New York, fetch prices in the thousands today, so you can see that quality is a good investment.

This chapter will explain simple lamp skills, many of them in common use seventy years ago. We hope to encourage the use of methods that will stand the test of time even with very easy lamps and to discourage some of the practices that have given stained glass lamps such

Leaded opalescent shade by Patrick Curran

"Trout Stream" by the Clows

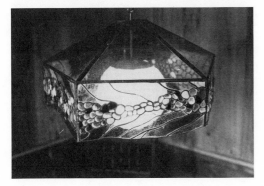

a poor reputation, particularly among decorators and interior designers.

Primary requirements are that lamps should be foiled and that they should be made of opalescent glass. The leaded opalescent lamp in the photo is an exception. It is made of European antique glass and it is definitely an "art piece." It required a light fixture within a light fixture to soften the electric light bulb. It illustrates the point that rules are made to be broken—if you know what you are doing.

The pattern for the first lamp project (page 102) is a simple lamp of eight pieces of glass. The beauty of this lamp depends especially upon the beauty of the glass in it, so pick up some really grainy and streaky opalescent glass if you can. When you are selecting glass be very careful not to choose opal glass instead of opalescent. Opal glass is made of a clear or gem-colored antique base. Light will pass right through it, and it can be exquisite in lampshades once you know how to handle it. It is traditionally used for skies in landscapes. Opalescent glass is made from a milky base and obscures light. The lamp in the photos is made of American opalescent green that looks like lime sherbet.

To make this lamp, you need adhesive 3/16-inch copper foil, flux, scissors, iron, solder, copper sulfate crystals, glass, and construction paper. Two *templates* of construction paper must be made from the design on page 102. A *template* is a pattern of heavy paper or thin metal that is designed to be cut around many times. If you cut the pattern out of the book, be sure to tape in a little

Lamp

pocket with the templates in place, so the lamp can be made again.

In the photos on page 104, notice that pattern cutting with templates is completely different from cutting over the cartoon. It takes a lot of time to cut templates, but it is by far the fastest and most efficient method for repeated cutting of any kind. Spend a minute studying the photos of the templates laid out and traced upon the glass. Notice the various methods for saving glass and utilizing one cut line for two cuts. A felt-tip pen or an indelible ink pen draws well on glass. For maximum speed, all the template lines are drawn as in the photo, and all the cut lines in one direction are made before snapping any of the lines off. Cut lines in opposing directions will cause unplanned breakage.

Breaking off straight cut lines for lamp templates is different from tapping and breaking curved pieces. The best way to separate the score line is to snap the pieces off the table edge as in the photos. *Do not tap;* tapping causes bumps and bumps will cause trouble when you assemble the lamp. Running pliers can also be used for snapping off the lines without tapping, but a little bump will be left where the head of the pliers was placed. Groze that bump off carefully. Do not be afraid of your glass. Glass will break on its score line if the proper force is applied and there are no opposing forces. Hold the glass firmly on the table with the score line lined up exactly over the edge. Snap down quickly and firmly with your other hand, applying force evenly on the score line.

It will be necessary to tap the bottom curve of the four smaller pieces. After tapping it, break the piece off by

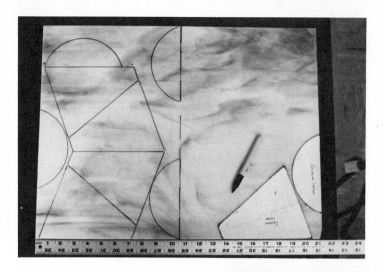

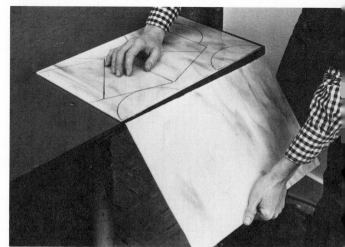

Lamp templates and snapping off

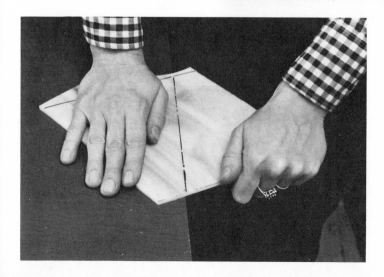

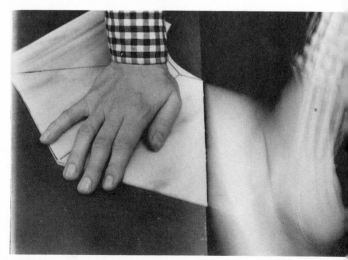

holding it in hand and pulling off the excess with the grozers. Usually the whole curve will separate nearly in one piece. Now, the eight pieces are cut.

Foil, flux, and tin each piece. (Three-sixteenths-inch adhesive foil is ideal for most opalescent templates.) Tack together the four larger pieces first. The easiest and most accurate way is to draw a perfect square with sides equal to the bottom of the templates. As with the lantern, line up two of the templates over the square, bend in the side seams as in the photo of the lamp, and fuse the seam. Assemble the other two pieces over the square. Then add a dab of solder to the eight joints for strength. Coat the inside and outside of the seams with flux and float them; the inside will be difficult. Be sure to prop the lamp so that the seams are level. Go slowly and be careful not to burn yourself. The outside bead of solder will be large, as in the photos, but it should be soldered until the outside bead is smooth and rounded.

Tack on the four skirt pieces, making sure that the corners line up. Make sure the angles created by the skirt pieces and the side pieces are all the same, and then fuse the bottom seam. Flux the bottom edge and float it. This bottom edge is strong enough for home use, but if you plan to sell the lamp, you would be wise to add a few extra strips of foil to the bottom edge for extra strength. Flux the other seam and float a bead on it similar to the bead on the side seams. See the photo of the finished lamp (page 106) for a standard.

For the vasecap, we used a 1-inch square of copper with a hole drilled in it. If you didn't make the lantern, read the section in the lantern chapter on supporting

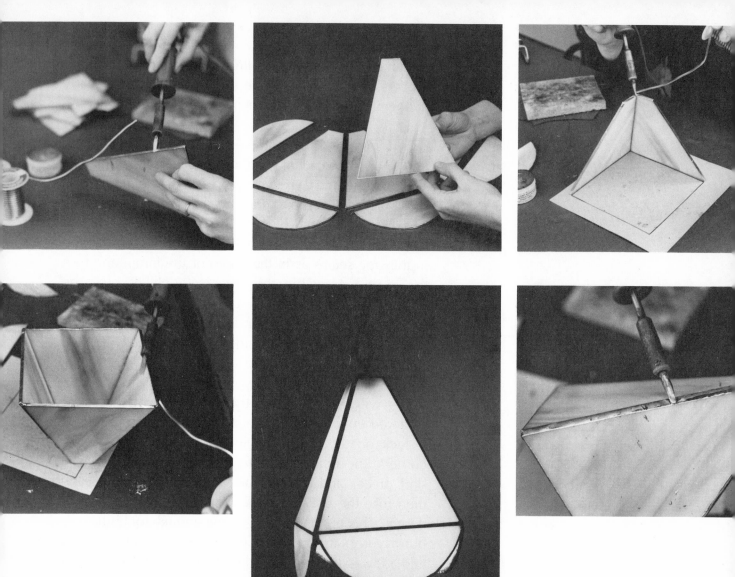

Soldering and assembling

lamps. If you want to have this lamp wired by someone else, you'll have to solder on the vasecap first.

Wipe the lamp vigorously with paper towels before you antique it. Notice what a sturdy little lamp it is! It will definitely stand the test of time. When deciding on a finish for the lamp, take into consideration the chain it will have. The lamp in the photo has a black chain; a strong mixture of tinner's fluid and copper sulfate turned the solder a chalky black. Experiment with finishes. Some glaziers use tinner's fluid, *antimony tri-chloride,* and some use heated ammonia and copper sulfate. For the final cleaning, immerse the lamp in warm soapy water and scrub it with a brush, working over the seams very thoroughly. Dry it and polish it with a rag.

The wiring diagram for the lantern (page 94) has all the instructions needed. Be sure that the two wires are firmly wrapped around the contact points in the socket. The top hook should be firmly screwed into the socket by itself or by a hex nut. Leave an inch of wire pulled out loosely in the chain so that the lamp is supported by the chain and not by the wires! This is especially important with large heavy shades. The small lamp is finished.

The second lamp design, the "Jugendstil Lamp," is drawn half to scale. It will have to be doubled by doubling measurements and then finding reference points within the design in order to copy the pattern. Don't be afraid to do this; it is easier than it seems. The *pantograph,* a drafting tool designed for enlarging designs, can be used, but drawing to scale is a skill you will need.

You are probably getting more ready all the time to try your own designs. With this lamp, simply reuse the

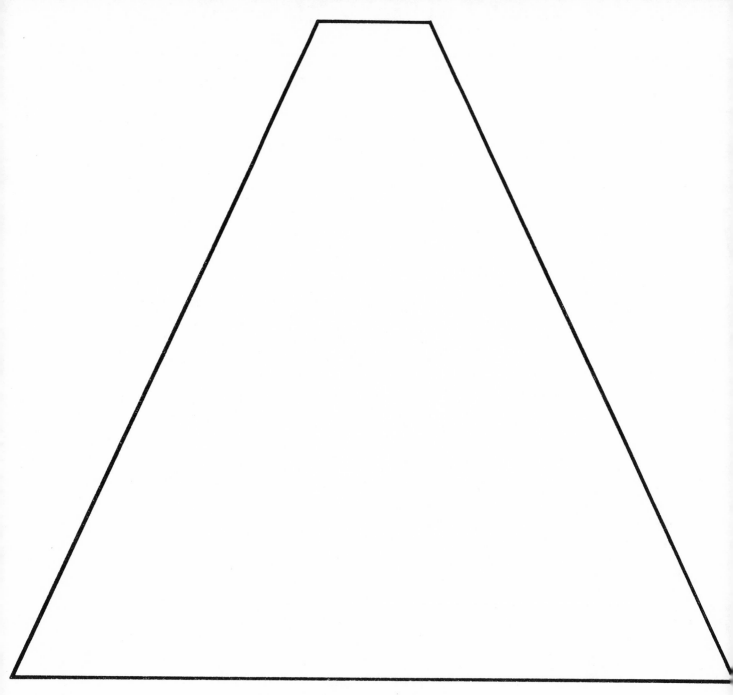

Top template for "Jugendstil"

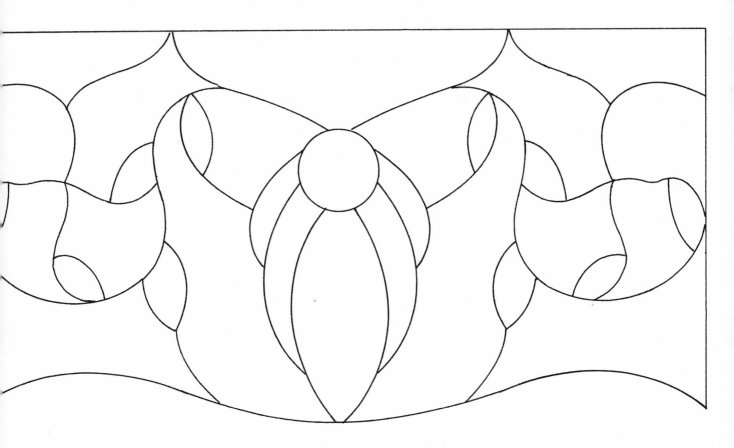

"Jugendstil" design, one-half to scale.

top six templates and make your own design for the six bottom pieces. This lamp is a good example of how intricate and delicate a construction lamp can be. Usually construction lamps are very simple in design. Lampmakers turn to mold lamps for complexity even though some lampmakers find themselves having a terrible time with mold lamps. (Mold lamp designing is covered extensively in the last chapter because it is an advanced skill.) A mold lamp isn't the only style that allows for complexity and intricacy, however. Almost anything can be designed with the basic model of the "Jugendstil Lamp." Imagine a six-sided thirties-style transportation lamp with planes in one panel, trains in another, boats, helicopters! A different type of flower could be represented in each panel! We call this the "Jugendstil Lamp" because it is made of eighty-year-old German satin glass (or frosted antique) that was made for the German art nouveau movement, the "Jugendstil." The glass was stored in a barn in Germany until 1973.

Constructed lamps can be designed with any number of templates and skirt pieces. Changing the width of a template section or the width of the angle of the templates in a construction lamp affects the number of templates in the top, and shortening the length of the template affects the diameter of the lamp. You must always make a cardboard model of a constructed lamp before you can be sure that a template is the right size. The cardboard model makes it easier to visualize the shape of the lamp and the working out of the skirt design. (The skirt is the bottom decorative row of a constructed lamp.) The model is frequently useful while assembling the lamp also. Be sure to save your templates! They represent hours of work.

Flowing lamp skirt with three repeats

It is possible to design a skirt for a constructed lamp that flows around the lamp rather than bending at every joint. The lamp in the photo has three repeats in the skirt. Usually a lamp of this type has 16 to 24 templates in the top, so that the angle of each bend in the skirt is lessened. The effect is much like working with a circle, but each bend point has to have a corresponding bend line in the skirt. The line can be curved around the end of a petal or leaf, but the line must begin where the bend point in the top matches up with the skirt. This is done by first making a cardboard model of the lamp top. The lamp in the photo also has lateral cuts, which strengthen a lamp because of extra soldering joints; they are more labor but are attractive. Next, a cardboard strip must be cut that will fit the bottom. (Several pieces of cardboard will have to be taped together for this.) The cardboard strip is lined up with the bottom line of the lamp top, and each bend mark is drawn onto the strip. Then the flowing design is drawn with the bend marks built into it. Pattern pieces are cut off the strip and the strip is taped to the lamp model for later construction. The glass is cut around the pattern pieces because these lamps are traditionally repetitive. If you make a nonrepetitive skirt, then you can make a pattern for the light table and it will go very fast. The variety of designs that can be done using this concept is infinite.

 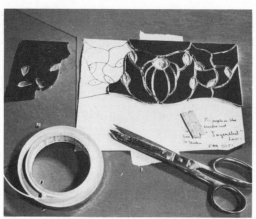 

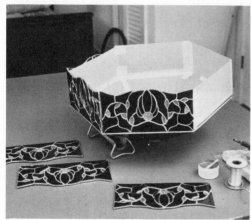 

The "Jugendstil"

Making the "Jugendstil Lamp"

Construct a cardboard mold of the lamp. Cut the glass for the six bottom sections over the light table. Line the pieces up in formation as you work in order to avoid confusion. Foil the pieces, using the thinnest foil possible. Tack together the bottom section pieces over the pattern, being very careful to have the sections *exactly* the same size as the pattern. Float all the bottom sections and clean them thoroughly with ammonia and a toothbrush. Cut the six top templates as accurately as possible. Foil the six top pieces with relatively thick foil for strength. Tin the pieces, fuse together the top, making use of the cardboard mold if it is helpful. If your mold turns out perfectly, you can fuse the top pieces inside the mold, which makes it easier. Our mold in the photos turned out a little small and the six top sections are being fused on top of it. If this lamp were more complicated, we would have had to make a new mold before proceeding further. After fusing the top six pieces, float and strengthen the top. You will find the top will be somewhat unstable until the bottom is attached. You will be nervous floating it! Strengthen it by adding extra strips of copper to the bottom joints and running an extra strip of copper all around the top hole. Support the lamp in your lap, in a box, on a mold, any way that works. This is the difficult stage in making this lamp. For mass production, all sorts of ingenious mold and support systems have been worked out.

The top is finished. If your mold worked out perfectly, set the top in the mold and attach the sides within the mold. In the photos you'll see that our mold was still useful, despite being too small. The mold is only a guide but a very necessary one.

The difficulty in attaching the skirt is that the angle of the skirt pieces might be off. Fuse the six skirt pieces on all sides and float the new seams. Again, you will have problems supporting the lamp as you work. Those seams must be level. The lamp will be stronger when the side pieces are added. Check the lamp very carefully, making sure all the seams are neatly floated. Put a lighted electric light bulb underneath the shade and check all the lines in the skirt. If there is any light coming through any seams, repair that seam with extra foil and refloat the seam.

Follow the instructions for wiring on page 115. The top hole in the "Jugendstil Lamp" is about 3 inches in diameter. For support, a piece of copper sheeting is soldered into the hole with a hole cut for wiring parts. The copper sheeting is tacked on, then a hex nut and chain are pulled through the hole and the lamp is hung to see if it is level. If the center hole for wiring parts is at all off-center, the lamp will tilt. Be very careful to balance it. When the lamp is level, solder on the copper sheeting or whatever other means of support you have for the lamp. Antique the lamp and clean it before you wire it. Notice how strong the lamp is now that it is all together! You can wash it in the yard with a hose or in the bathtub. Enjoy.

A complicated construction lamp is as difficult to make as a mold lamp, but designing for mold lamps is

Wiring inside a lamp

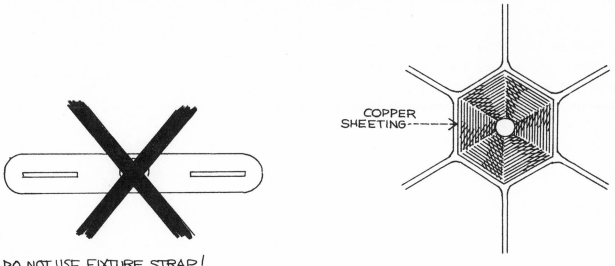

DO NOT USE FIXTURE STRAP!

COPPER SHEETING----→

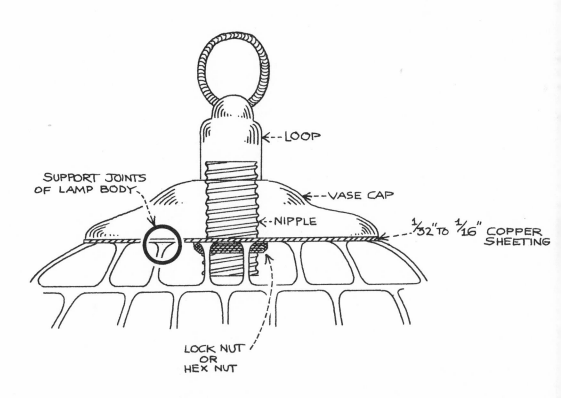

LOOP

SUPPORT JOINTS OF LAMP BODY----

←--VASE CAP

←-NIPPLE

1/32" TO 1/16" COPPER SHEETING

LOCK NUT OR HEX NUT

Wiring a larger lamp

so difficult that most glaziers depend upon patterns ordered from suppliers. The last chapter attempts to give some instruction on mold lamp designing and describe some of the exciting experimental trends in contemporary glass.

Chapter Five

Advanced Methods

Each stained glass specialty requires a lifetime of study. Seventy years ago, when stained glass work was much more specialized than it is today, each person working in the studio tended to do one job—one was a pattern cutter, another a glass cutter, another a foil wrapper, another a glazier, and there was a head designer. Designers rarely executed their own works and this is still the case in many large studios today. Specialty work (bending glass, etching, beveling, or pressing jewels) was usually done overseas, and standard sizes and colors of parts were ordered and stocked by the studios. The German, Austrian, Italian, and Belgian companies that did specialty work in the nineteenth century have either gone out of business or switched to making less individualized products. It is almost impossible now to get beveled or etched parts, or a variety of interesting jewels. We tried to find people still working in one of the special areas in order to gather general information for the benefit of persons interested in pursuing one of the specialties as an independent artist. We asked these craftsmen to make a contribution to our book.

We considered a variety of skills: painting and firing, staining and firing, beveling, glass making, large window construction, mold designing, glass bending, glass etching, and *dalles de verre* work. Painting and firing and large window construction are not covered in this book because the definitive work on the subject was written by Patrick Reyntiens in *The Techniques of Stained Glass,* mentioned in the bibliography. Also, large window construction is beyond the scope of this book, and we do have a somewhat negative attitude toward painting on glass. Somehow the blocking of light caused by the paint on the surface seems to defeat the purpose of stained glass. Beveling is not discussed because straight beveling is now done by a machine that costs in the excess of $50,000. Beveling is an industrial art, and the grinding and polishing turned many a young man into an old man much too soon during the nineteenth century. Here is a case where machines have liberated mankind. We would still have loved to cover curved beveling, but the equipment outlay is exorbitant and the work very crushing. We also chose not to cover making glass. The cost of glass ovens and annealing ovens, and the present-day costs of fuel make it almost impossible for the individual artist to make glass. If you want specialty glass, get to know a glassblower who already has some of the equipment problems solved, or worm your way into a school where you might be able to use some of the equipment.

Bending glass is covered because it is fairly simple to do, and it can be an essential part of lamp making. Those of you who do invest in a kiln will probably also wish to paint or stain glass. Mr. Reyntiens' book will be most helpful, and Jack Trompetter is doing some exciting work staining glass, which is covered at the end of this chapter. *Dalles de verre* technique is discussed because this method lends itself so well to free-form design and abstract statements. It is tactile, requires a small outlay for tools, and is a technique that hasn't yet captured the imagination of the hobbyist. Etching is extensively covered because it is a highly pleasurable small-muscle activity and affords great intricacy. Some new methods have been developed since Mr. Reyntiens wrote about it.

Making a mold lamp and problems of mold designing are the next challenge after learning how to make complicated constructed lamps like the "Jugendstil." There are many mold lamp methods to consider. We prefer using Styrofoam molds but sometimes use plaster of paris section molds, and we would use wood molds if we could afford them. Tiffany used hardwood molds at Tiffany Studios in New York. Molds have two or three surface curves, and it is very difficult to visualize and execute designs on them. A simple cone mold is not included in this category because cone molds are not really any more difficult than constructed lamps. A cone mold is simply 16 to 24 templates that have a slight side-to-side curve, but there is no curve from top to bottom.

We have not yet found the perfect solution for doing original designs on curved molds. It is possible that the perfect solution does not exist. Often the bugs are worked out on the first lamp, and the second lamp can be made without much adjustment. Patterns are available which fit the most popular sized Styrofoam and pressed foam section molds. These patterns still require adjusting. Before attempting mold design, remember to check yourself constantly as you work along. A design that is $\frac{1}{16}$ inch off will not show on the first section, but the design will be off as much as ¼ inch after three or four sections. Correct yourself at this point and remember that it is almost impossible not to be off on the first lamp. You may well be tempted to give up on design and buy the patterns. We really feel, though, that it is much better to do something original in most cases; even an adaptation of an old lamp is more interesting than following a pattern, and we have not seen great results from pattern-making by individual artists. There *are* a few small companies specializing in exquisite copies of Tiffany originals, and you will find it *very* hard to compete with those companies.

The first step in mold design is to section off the mold. Place the mold on a large clear piece of paper, draw a circle around the mold, and then remove the mold. With a protractor, section the circle into sixteen equal parts. This circle represents the flat plane of the mold in sixteen sections. (Don't worry; I can't visualize the mold surface either, even though I was excellent in geometry.) Draw the sixteen lines out beyond your circle so the lines will be visible when the mold is placed back on the circle. Place the mold back on the circle. Mark the bottom of the mold with indelible ink at each one of the sixteen lines so that the mold can be lined up properly on the circle if it slides while you're working with it.

Examine the first photo of work being done on the mold lamp (page 124). Notice the lines extending out at the base of the mold. A line is being drawn down the side of the mold with indelible ink along the side of a strip of copper foil taped to the exact center of the mold top and to the side of one of the section lines at the mold bottom. The foil is being pressed into the curve of the mold as the line is being drawn. String instead of foil, pinned into the center of the top, is also great for doing this. Go around the mold with the string or strip of foil, working from the exact center of the top down to each section line. The mold is drawn into sixteen sections so that the design can be broken down enough for visualization and for accuracy checks during assembly after cutting. We draw all over our molds, as you can see in the photos. The same section size can be used for many lamp designs, or the same mold can be sectioned off into three or six parts with red or green ink. We don't worry about drawing all over the molds because the mold is $\frac{1}{50}$ or less of the completed lamp cost and the designs are so hard to visualize. Also, a Styrofoam mold won't last through more than six assemblies because solder burns into the Styrofoam. You may ruin one mold per lamp assembly. You can protect the mold surface with masking tape.

After the mold is sectioned off, cut a template that exactly matches $\frac{1}{16}$ of the lamp surface. Cut it and trim it until it is perfect, then try it on the mold for accuracy. Move it around the mold section by section. If the template is not accurate, you'll find yourself getting off after a few sections. Adjust the template and move into the next section, drawing lines on the side of the template as you move around. Usually you'll get it cut to the perfect size by the time you're into the third section.

As in the illustration on the left, draw the template side by side four times on a piece of design paper that can be seen through easily on the light table. That drawing represents one quarter-section of the lamp surface

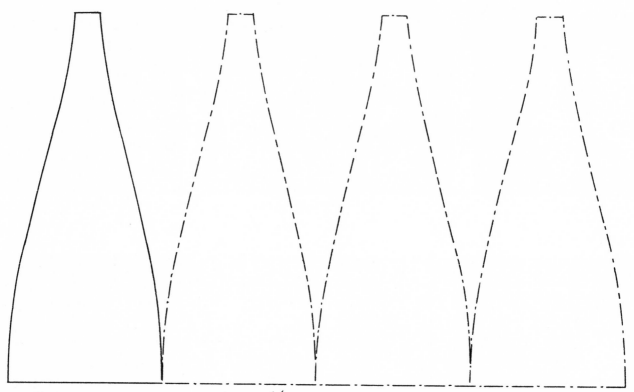

FOUR TEMPLATES — FLAT PLANE O $^1/4$ OF LAMP SURFACE IF CUT OUT AND DOTTED LINES CONNECTED.

Working with mold lamp template

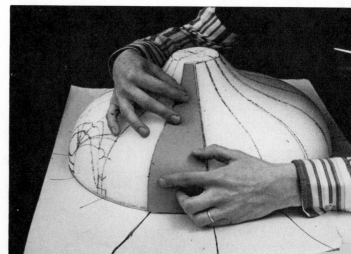

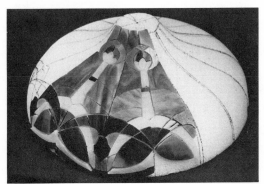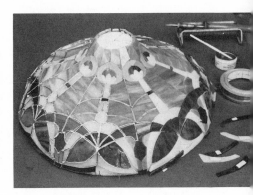

Doing a mold lamp

laid out flat. Taped to the mold with the dotted lines matching up, the section will mold to the curve of the quarter-section. You can work out your design on the quarter-section taped to the mold or lying flat.

The books on stained glass which discuss mold designing or have lamp projects advise you to cut patterns for lampmaking, and the pressed foam quarter-section molds sometimes have patterns enclosed. As with leadwork, pattern cutting is just too time-consuming. This is especially true if you are making a nonrepetitive lamp. Nonrepetitive lamps are incredibly difficult and very rare, and one of these days somebody is going to come along who can visualize the whole curved surface of a mold as if it were flat, and that person will be able to make a nonrepeating mold lamp as if the lamp were no more complicated than a square surface area. Mr. Curran, mentioned later in the chapter, spent a great deal of time thinking about how the map-makers deal with transposing a curved surface to a flat plane and felt the answer might be found by pursuing the mathematical formulas for map-making. Anyway, cut the lamp over the light table. The lamp in the photos, quite intricate, was cut in twenty hours.

For cutting, set the mold right next to the light table with a roll of masking tape. As in the third photo, each piece is taped to the mold after it is cut. This prevents loss and confusion. When all the pieces are cut, the lamp is ready to be foiled. Remove one piece at a time, foil it, flux it and tack it together so that the foil will not darken. Foiled pieces begin to darken about a week after they are stuck on the lamp, and they are more difficult to flux and solder. Finish foiling, tacking, and floating the whole lamp. It's very time-consuming but *very* satisfying. The vase cap, wiring instructions, and antiquing are the same as for the "Jugendstil." This project probably will take you a few months, but what a lamp!

Designing and Making a Lamp on Pressed Foam Quarter- or Sixth-Section Molds

The design procedure is the same as with a Styrofoam mold. For a quarter-section basic sixteen-template lamp like the Styrofoam mold in the photos, section off the quarter-section into four parts, using a full drawn circle on paper. The circle will come in handy when you are ready to connect the finished four quarter-sections. Cut the template, check and recheck it, draw around the template four times in order to get a flat plane of the mold surface for designing. Adapt the design given as your example for the Styrofoam or make your own design. After you get the design all worked out on paper, copy it. Then cut between the noncontiguous sides of the flat-plane quarter-section, the *dotted lines* in the illustration for the Styrofoam mold, and tape the extra design to the pressed foam mold. You have to do this because you cannot draw easily on the foam mold, and the design will keep you in place on the mold. (Your mold will come with these instructions anyway.) From here on the only difference between the Styrofoam mold and the pressed one is that you cut and foil a quarter of the lamp at a time. Tack the sections when they are finished, float them for strength, and fuse the four sections over the circle that was drawn for sectioning off the mold. Some molds come with pattern pieces, and the pattern stamped on the mold, as in the photo. We feel that the pattern pieces are too time-consuming. This manufacturer also advises holding the foiled glass in place with pins while tacking sections. Tape is easier and you can reuse the mold. Pins are hard on it.

When we went up to Vermont to visit Mr. Schneider to find out all about bending glass, he also showed us his ingenious method for making plaster of paris molds. Mr. Schneider apprenticed during the twenties with John Dittenger from Austria at Art Leaded Glass, Baldwin, Long Island. With great sadness, Mr. Dittenger had to let Mr. Schneider go because of the depression, and Mr. Schneider did commercial glazing in New York City for many years until he retired in Vermont and began working with stained glass again.

Mr. Schneider's mold-making method would be of great use to anyone making lamps, and particularly to someone dissatisfied with the stock sizes of commercial molds. A rudder spun in a bed of plaster is the basis of his method. The rudder must be adjusted to size for the proper curve and diameter of the desired shade. The rudder is slotted into a 1½-inch dowel (a clothes closet dowel is ideal), and the dowel is gripped in a block of wood nailed to the ceiling. Examine the photo (at right). The block of wood must grip the dowel enough to hold it, but be loose enough so that the dowel can spin. The mold is spun manually in a sturdy wooden box

packed with wet sand or sawdust lined with enough plaster of paris to make a 1½-inch-thick mold. Plaster can be purchased in hundred-pound bags. Build the packing material to the approximate shape, allowing for the 1½-inch plaster of paris, before pouring in the plaster. The box can be reused for making many molds, and the rudder and pattern should be stored together for other lamps. The mold will begin to set as you spin around the rudder in about a half hour. The rudder can be raised at that point and the mold should sit in place overnight. Invite a child over to watch you spin the mold. Children love this sort of thing!

The lamp is built *inside* the plaster of paris mold. Designing for the inside of the mold involves the same principles as designing for the outside of the Styrofoam mold. The inside surface must be divided into quarter- or sixth-sections, depending upon the number of repeats in the lamp design, and an accurate template must be made for the basic design. Check your template constantly and be prepared for adjustments. Mr. Schneider said he is always making adjustments on the first lamp. Cut the pieces for the top first. After you've cut a few inches, foil the pieces, put them in place against the top rim, and tack them in place. You cannot tape easily to plaster of paris, but the glass almost lies in place in the mold. This is a disadvantage, but Mr. Schneider achieves great accuracy and speed with this method. Mr. Schneider is a fine technician, as you can see from the photo of a lamp that was built on the inside of one of his spun molds. The finishing process is the same as with any mold lamp.

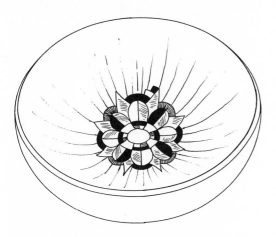

Building a lamp inside a mold

Bending Glass

While we're with Mr. Schneider, we'll go into bending glass. Glass is lovely when it is bent. Bent panels are beautiful by themselves as a lamp of four to eight panels, or they are lovely as the top body of a curved shade with an intricate colorful skirt. If you do have a kiln available, bending the top four to eight panels for a large shade is actually quite a labor-saver. Then designing the skirt is very much like designing the skirt for a construction shade of sixteen to twenty-four panels discussed in Chapter Four. It is possible to imagine a myriad of contemporary designs made with bent glass.

The lamp by Mr. Schneider

The Kiln

It is possible to use a top-loading or front-loading kiln. A front-loading kiln is easier to work with particularly if you can elevate it four feet. The kiln box should be at least 18 inches square for firing more than one panel at a time. For staining and firing or bending more than one panel, you will need stacking shelves. It is wise to buy them when purchasing the kiln. The kiln should be capable of firing up to 1,800 degrees even though you'll rarely go above 1,300 degrees. A pyrometer is almost a necessity for firing with glass. The pyrometer will give a reading on the temperature in the kiln.

Making a Mold for Bending a Panel

Making a mold for an original-size panel of glass requires the spinning of a plaster of paris mold, and the cutting of the mold into four to eight sections with a saw, depending upon the panel size and bend. The majority of situations will call for bending a panel to match a panel of an existing size. The photo at left is of Mr. Schneider making a new mold, using an old bent panel as a model. If the panel you wish to duplicate is cracked, it can still be utilized if you glue the crack back together. Mr. Schneider made a box of wood that was slightly wider and longer than the panel and was about 4 or 5 inches deep. Two inches of wet sand or sawdust is packed into the box firmly by hand, with a curve that approximates the bend of the panel. The panel is placed on the packing material but not pressed into it. An indentation is made into the packing material above the narrow top of the panel, which will result in the ridge of plaster above the top of the panel that is visible in the photos. When the newly cut piece of glass is lying flat on the mold in the kiln and begins to bend downward, the ridge keeps the glass in place on the mold. Before pouring the plaster of paris onto the bent panel lying on the packing, coat the glass surface with salad oil or motor oil to keep the plaster of paris from sticking to the glass. Pour 2 inches of plaster carefully into the mold and let it set for one-half hour. Then pry off the wooden sides with a hammer, brush sawdust off the back of the mold, and the result is the glass sitting in the plaster with the ridge above the top. Scrape saw-

![Glass in plaster]

Glass in plaster

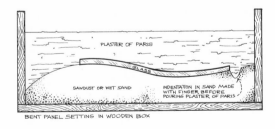

Panel setting in plaster of paris

dust and excess plaster off the edges of the glass with a lead knife, as Mr. Schneider is doing in the photo. Remove the panel very carefully by picking it up with the tip of the lead knife. Clean up and smooth out the mold as in the photo, and let it sit overnight before firing. This mold is useful for only one firing. For repeated firings, follow the same procedure with gauging plaster. It is cheaper than plaster of paris, but has to be sifted because it has small stones in it, and will have to be shipped on order. Your hardware man can probably order it or tell you where to write for it.

Cleaning mold

Cutting the Glass to Fit the Mold Size

Simply make a pattern that matches the original piece of glass, or lay a piece of paper in the plaster of paris mold after it's finished and draw a pattern to size. Cut the piece of glass to be fired *perfectly* to size. It is wise to avoid *any* cutting or grozing after firing because the glass may be brittle. Besides, you'd hate to crack a piece of glass after you've fired it.

Firing

We thought firing was complicated, but we found there is no reason to be afraid of it. If you know the

132

bending temperature of the glass you are firing, kiln cones can be used to trip off the kiln once it has reached temperature. Mr. Schneider said that generally reds bend at 1,200 degrees, blues and greens at 1,250 degrees, and yellows and ambers at 1,300 degrees. But Mr. Schneider uses one manufacturer's opalescent glass, and each glass type and color must be monitored until you have a sense of the bending temperature. Even if you overfire a bit, you will not ruin the glass. Overfiring will destroy the shine on the surface of opalescent glass, and extreme overfiring will cause little cracks in the surface. Then beyond that, it'll melt.

Place the mold on kiln-stacking stilts as in the photo, shut the top and turn it on. It will reach temperature in about a half hour. Mr. Schneider is opening the kiln for the camera after it has reached temperature and adjusting the glass on the mold with a metal rod. Always check the glass as it is bending because it can slide off the mold when it first begins to move. You don't have to worry much about opening the kiln while firing. You must be more careful when firing painted or stained glass, especially if the room where the kiln sits is drafty. Annealing is also simpler when bending than when painting and staining. Simply let the kiln reach temperature, turn it off, and let it cool overnight. Mr. Schneider even put a stacking triangle in the lid to cause the panel in the photos to cool in two to four hours. This is not possible when firing painted or stained pieces. Opalescent glass is very durable. Each firing costs about 75 cents.

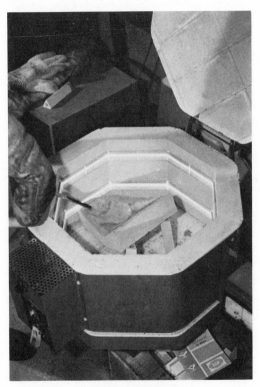

Prodding the mold

Making Molds for Fruit

Follow the above procedure with the wooden box, packing material, placing in the glass fruit to be duplicated, oiling the fruit, and pouring in the plaster of paris. In a given mold, place three to six different fruits side by side. The danger with copying commercially made bent fruit is that your shades may have a commercial look to them. Original designs of raised birds, new flower designs, anything, really, can be made by raising a design on the packing material, thereby causing an indentation in the plaster of paris. Your imagination is the only limit. We have seen art nouveau shades with three hundred to five hundred bent pieces in them that are magnificent.

Dalles de Verre

Rodger Chamberlain is a free-form artist working with *dalles de verre* in his studio at Orleans, Massachusetts. He was a landscape architect from 1930 to 1957. He began working with glass in the late fifties. Before going into a description of his method, let me quote his last letter to me: "But I have yet to see any of the young doing much more with *dalles de verre,* and I wonder at it, for it is a wonderful medium of expression."

Slabs of one-inch-thick glass were first made in France

Work by Rodger Chamberlain

Work by Rodger Chamberlain

in the thirties, called *dalles de verre*. The term remained un-Anglicized. They have been made in the United States for about twenty years, and they are most commonly used here in large windows weighing tons. Windows of this type are ideal for huge buildings. The *dalles de verre* window wall is very strong, it is not dwarfed by the large structures, and it looks very well with modern building materials such as pressed concrete and steel. The glass in *dalles de verre* window walls for huge buildings is usually cut to size according to a cartoon and cemented in. This subject is excellently covered by Mr. Reyntiens, and obviously windows of this type are beyond the scope of this book. Mr. Chamberlain's descriptions of working with *dalles de verre* are for smaller pieces, and his method requires a lot of handwork.

135

Mr. Chamberlain prefers to play with the glass, first making each piece a work of art by cutting it and faceting it. Then he works with all the faceted pieces on the light table, letting the glass suggest form and color. In the photos you can see that his results are abstract, organic, suggestive, and original. The uncut *dalles* are about 1 inch thick and 8 by 12 inches. Mr. Chamberlain scores the glass on each side with a cutter, and he breaks the *dalle* to size by bringing it down sharply on a steel wedge or striking the score with a shingler's hammer. *Dalles* are traditionally chipped with a dalles hammer, and this is termed *knapping*. Mr. Chamberlain likes to chip the *dalles* with a shingler's hammer, which sends the chips to the right if you're right-handed, or to the left if you're left-handed. He also crushes segments of the *dalles* with a geologist's mortar and pestle, making interesting small facets. After he gets enough faceted pieces of glass for a planned work, he is ready to assemble on the light table.

Before assembling, the framing problems must be completely or partially solved. If the piece is to be a window of a specific size, then the frame must be made ahead of time so that the *dalles de verre* composition fits into the frame size. If the piece is to hang in a window, then the frame can be made later. For a specific size, a box is made of flat lead and soldered at the corners. Then a ribbon of copper wire is soldered to the inside of the leaded box. Between the joints, the copper wire is pulled inward so that the matrix of the *dalles de verre* piece sets around the loop, making the frame and piece a whole. A copper loop is brought out of the top of the lead box for hanging. If the *dalles de verre* piece

Rodger Chamberlain working at Orleans, Mass.

is to be a window, the loop can be dispensed with and the lead box can be framed in wood.

Having made the lead box or having in mind the relative size of the piece, Mr. Chamberlain is ready to form the faceted *dalles* on the light table as in the photo. The light table surface is carefully waxed periodically with paste wax to prevent sticking. The light table is lit with a 48-inch Macbeth fluorescent tube, which renders the closest approximation to natural light. Even after forming has occurred on the light table, the first awareness of a piece as an artistic success occurs when the piece is held up to receive the sunlight. With the *dalles* on the light table, Mr. Chamberlain said, ''I prefer working freely with the glass, letting the shapes, forms and colors suggest design, reshaping pieces when necessary. Stained glass in place, I sift black sand between the pieces, immediately forcing light through the glass. Any final change is now made and then I spoon polyester resin, with catalyst added, carefully between the pieces, soaking into the sand, more resin, more sand, keeping a firm consistency to required thickness of ⅝ inch to ¾ inch.'' Polyester resin and catalyst can be purchased at a hobby store or a stained glass supplier who also carries *dalles*. The lead frame with copper wire looped inside it is placed around the formed *dalles* before the pouring of sand and resin. The outside edge between the *dalles* and the frame can be 1 inch to 5 or 6 inches. After the sand and resin have been poured, the hardening time depends upon the temperature in the studio and the amount of catalyst added. On hot days Mr. Chamberlain works fast, because otherwise the resin will harden before he can use it all. Unhardened resin can be cleaned up with acetone, and hardened resin dropped on the glass will snap off if struck with a knife blade.

The faceted sides of the *dalles* are meant to be turned inward because the flat side catches the light. The faceted side of a *dalles de verre* window is likely to leak. *Dalles de verre* is a method rarely used by the hobbyist, and avenues of supply are hard to solve. (See the Appendix for supply problems.) Each *dalle* is expensive but one *dalle* makes many facets. Six *dalles* of six different colors would be enough to make a start. If you want to make a small *dalles de verre* window, it would be wise for you to read Mr. Reyntiens' section on *dalles de verre* in case steel reinforcement rods are needed in your window.

We tend to agree with Mr. Chamberlain that working with faceted *dalles de verre* is an exciting hobby that is very close to doing sculpture. It is tactile, it can be very free-form, and there is something about the quality of colors in the *dalles* from the thickness of the glass that reminds one of medieval glass.

Etching

The traditional etching method is to coat the glass with melted beeswax, scrape away the beeswax where etching is to be done, soak the coated glass in hydrofluoric acid until the acid has etched the exposed parts, and then remove the beeswax. This method was especially popular during the Victorian era, when floral and nature detail was the rage. Etching can assuage the great frustration that most glaziers feel about not being able to get enough detail with leaded or foiled work. Like the painter, the glazier also wants flowing tresses of hair, the delicate curves of the female form, or the murkiness of pond life in late summer. German artists managed to carry this desire for detail to extremes during the Victorian era when they made beaded curtain window screens of intricate patterns, and archway screens out of designs of millions of tiny translucent gem-colored beads. I've seen only hazy photos of these astonishing beaded pieces, and I would not believe they had ever been made if I hadn't reached the same point of frustration myself just before I apprenticed for glass. I made a copy of a Caucasian oriental rug in a wooden frame by assembling two-millimeter translucent beads on filament. (A two-millimeter bead is the size of a pinhead.)

Etching by sandblasting gives Patrick Curran the precision, the detail, the perfection he strives for in glass. Jack Trompetter wanted the detail and he wanted it to be multicolored. I thought of Joseph's desire for a robe of many colors when I first saw Jack's mandala window.

Jack etches flashed glass. Then he stains and fires the etched pieces. Those of you who are frustrated by the limits of copper foil and leadwork, are intrigued by the detail possible in oil painting, and yet are hopelessly frustrated by the back of the canvas (you want light!) but don't want to paint on glass may be able to solve the dilemma by etching and even staining and firing etched glass.

Etching by sandblasting

Patrick Curran was asked to contribute his sandblasting method because the method is not covered in print so far as we know. We also wanted Pat represented in the book because he is a mad inventor—of sorts. This method is one of many new techniques he is working on in his basement, and Pat's work is a good example of the wide-ranging experimentation going on today with stained glass.

Patrick Curran's Sandblasting Technique for Etching Glass: "To etch glass using this method, first mask the piece to be etched with a vinyl or plastic tape (adhesive-backed). Contact ® paper works very well. Using an Exacto knife, cut out the areas of the tape that are to be exposed to the sandblast so that you will have cut a

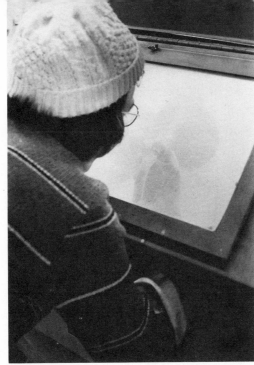

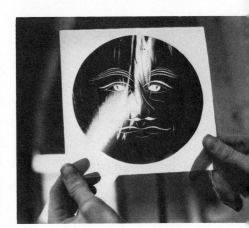

Patrick Curran sandblasting

plastic stencil on the glass. The difficulty of this process is locating the right sandblasting equipment to do the blasting. Mold and tool companies use this equipment for cleaning molds, and you can ask them to use the equipment. The purchasing cost of this type of equipment would be prohibitive for doing etching as a craft. The equipment functions as follows: The box is completely enclosed with heavy rubber gloves protruding inside to protect the hands during the process. (See photo.) A heavy-duty vacuum draws out the dust on the side and there is a trap at the bottom which collects the unused abrasive.

"Depending upon the corrosiveness of the grit being used, the frosted or etched sections will have a rougher or smoother surface. For example, 100 grit is used for heavy work blasting such as etching on mortuary stones, and 220 grit—aluminum oxide—is a fine abrasive and renders a smooth etched surface on glass. There are two hoses in the box which are joined to a gun or nozzle. One hose carries compressed air of approximately 90 lbs. pressure per sq. inch. The other hose leads to the sump or trap at the bottom of the box. When the compressed air is released, it comes out the nozzle causing a vacuum in the other hose which draws out the abrasive grit at a high velocity. The grit then mixes with the compressed air coming out the nozzle. The abrasive grit strikes the surface of the glass, chipping away at the surface. The particles bounce off the vinyl. The compressed air is released by a foot pedal on the floor which is attached to the air hose.

"Flashed antique can be used to best advantage with this process. The flashing is etched away in a design creating one piece of glass with two colors. Flashed

The Mandala Window by Jack Trompetter

Manadala Window detail

glass comes blue on yellow, red on blue, blue on green, red on yellow, green on yellow, and all colors on clear glass. As in the photos, a Contact paper design can be reused by taping over the design with masking tape, and removing the design from the glass carefully with an Exacto knife.''

The last technique to be covered is etching and then staining and firing etched glass. Staining glass is not to be confused with painting glass. Glass stains react molecularly with the surface of the glass. Staining does not obfuscate light—our objection to painting on glass.

Jack Trompetter was a commercial designer for The Big Apple in New York City for ten years. The mandala window in the photos was made by Jack and a friend, Claire Von Peski, both of South Amherst, Massachusetts, in 1973. It is Jack's first adventure in stained glass. I was asked to approve the mandala window for the Fall Show at Leverett, Massachusetts, in 1974, and I was literally shocked when I walked in the room to view it. Black and white photography does not do it justice. It is etched, flashed, stained, of reds, yellows, blues, clears, greens, and is remarkably sophisticated. We felt that a little bit of Jack's obsession with glass, his special excitement about light and color, comes through in his statement about his work and his own illustrations.

Etching and Staining
by Jack Trompetter:

''I'm intrigued by this method of creating images with colored glass because it is close to the sensibility I have for painting and drawing. I feel that etched stained glass has all the freedom and grace of movement, depth, clarity, and brightness of any painting, drawing or sculpture. And it plays with the sun. I learned it from Ron Klaren of Chelsea, Vermont. Apparently many stained glass craftsmen do not use this method, either out of ignorance or for technical reasons; one being that the thin flash surface wears with the weather. I made my windows so that the flash side faces in, to protect it from weary weather and so that the viewer can see and touch the glass and dig the different levels of the etch. Instead of using iron crossbars to support the structural strength of the window, which contrast with the design if you make shapes other than right angles, I use Plexiglas, protecting the window in the process. [See illustration.]

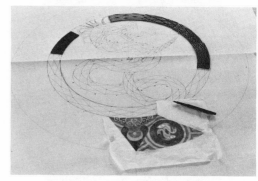

Design in works by Jack

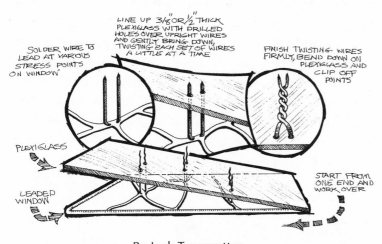

SOLDER WIRE TO LEAD AT VARIOUS STRESS POINTS ON WINDOW

LINE UP 3/8" OR 1/2" THICK PLEXIGLASS WITH DRILLED HOLES OVER UPRIGHT WIRES AND GENTLY BRING DOWN, TWISTING EACH SET OF WIRES A LITTLE AT A TIME

FINISH TWISTING WIRES FIRMLY, BEND DOWN ON PLEXIGLASS AND CLIP OFF POINTS

PLEXIGLASS

LEADED WINDOW

START FROM ONE END AND WORK OVER

By Jack Trompetter

"After the glass has been cut to shape, I cut out of Contact ® Transparent sticky-back (bought in rolls at any decent hardware store) 2 pieces to the shape of the

By Jack Trompetter

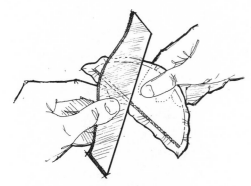

Jack working

glass with a ½" lip, and apply the tape to both sides of the glass, rubbing it down with my fingers to prevent air pockets. Then using the edge of another piece of glass like a very sharp file, I gently separate the lip on each side from the rest of the Contact-covered glass. [See second illustration.]

"Now that my design is drawn to full scale and glass cut to shape, I trace each area that will subsequently be a piece of etched flashed glass on a piece of frosted tracing paper, using a fine black felt-tipped pen. That piece of tracing paper goes on a light table, on top of which I put the piece of transparent Contact-covered glass taped to the tracing paper. With a #2 Exacto blade, I cut the design on the Contact-covered *flash side of the glass.* The Contact is plastic and acid-resistant, as far as hydrofluoric acid is concerned. This acid will eat glass, wood, stone, concrete, you and your friends, if you don't treat it with respect. After the design is cut with the Exacto knife, I peel off the Contact-covered areas where I want the acid to 'eat,' leaving the back and rest of the front covered. The more care you take in cutting, the clearer your etched areas will be. The acid bath that I use is approximately 15 percent acid, 85 percent water. It's easier, and in my opinion more attractive, to stain a piece of etched glass that is not pitted. Strong bath = fast and pitted; Weak bath = slow and clear. The warmer the weather, the faster the 'bite' and vice versa. I like to leave the pieces in overnight during the winter. The container should be of a hard plastic, and no more full than can be easily carried without spilling. The only thing hydrofluoric acid doesn't seem to eat is plastic; very organic, that acid. Put the piece in the bath, read a book, sing a song, come back and check the bath, rub the finely eaten glass off your piece with a feather (don't tend to pick off the Contact edges), and remember to keep washing the feather in another pail next to the bath. A good feather can be hard to come by. Wash yourself constantly. When I first started doing this I didn't pay enough respect to the power of the acid, didn't wash my hands after fooling around with it, was just plain stupid, and I had a burning sensation in my fingertips for days on end.* So take care, folks, keep the acid out of reach of the uninformed, and be clear about its usage and potential. Why, I knew a man who used to hang over his acid bath for so long that his eyeglasses got eaten up!

''Sometimes a piece of Contact will loosen off the glass, perfect it ain't, so you've got to pay attention. If this happens, take the glass out of the bath, rinse well and let it dry thoroughly. Reapply the Contact and continue.

''I have my bath outside so that the fumes have a place to dissipate. When the bath has done the job, using a pair of rubber-tipped tongs, take out the piece of glass, dunk it in a pail of water, bring it to a sink and rinse thoroughly. If, for example, your flash is blue on yellow, try not etching only down to the yellow, but try to get

Etched glass

---

*CAUTION: If you are working daily with hydrofluoric acid etching, even in weak solutions, wear household rubber gloves. If your fingers become dark under the nails, and *very* painful, soak them immediately in alcohol and iced water for some time, apply white petroleum jelly, and bandage them. Soaking in iced water to which baking soda or boric acid has been added is also helpful. If you should get a serious burn from full-strength acid, soak as above and apply magnesium oxide ointment (no prescription necessary) and bandage. See a doctor.

gradations of blue by taking it out of the bath sooner. Experiment!

Staining

"You need the stains, a good selection of sable brushes, a badger brush, a muller for grinding on, a #2 Exacto blade and handle, Contact paper, and access to an upright kiln. Cover the non-flash side of your glass with Contact and cut and peel away areas to be stained with the knife. Grind the stain powder, which comes in granulated form, on the frosted side of the plate glass with a few brushloads of water and the muller till the clumps are gone. The finer you grind it, the clearer and cleaner your eventual stain will fire. Apply the ground stain with the badger, evenly covering all of and more than your exposed areas with loose broad strokes. When the stain is dry, peel away the Contact carefully so as not to cause fissured areas. I've found that when I grind the stain down to just the right consistency and brush it on evenly, there are just about no fissures or missed areas.

"Put the glass in the kiln and fire away. Experiment before you fire a finished piece of glass. My first adventure with staining was with a piece of blue on clear that I wanted to stain yellow and red. I finally found that both colors fired best at 1,200 degrees for 5 minutes, then down to 1,000 degrees for 5 minutes. I usually fire in the late afternoon and let it cool down overnight. It's really exciting the next morning to find out how it turned out. It's also fascinating what happens in the kiln. The glass 'opens up' and lets the stain go through its changes below the surface of the glass, and the glass, while cooling down, closes over the stain. Molecular miscegenation. Unlike paints, which stay on the surface, susceptible to wear, the stain is more or less 'in' the glass. If, for example, you want a dark yellow appearance, you apply the stain and fire as many times as is needed. Or, if you want a green stain, stain successively yellow under blue glass. Experiment! As it is, I'm still learning more about the craft and its nuances. I recommend Patrick Reyntiens for more information on the mineral composition of glass and stains. Wash your hands after that acid and have fun, folks.''

Finished work

Sources of Supplies

Suppliers

The following are lists of suppliers for each major type of material or tool we use for stained glass work. We have dealt personally with only a selection of these suppliers; when we have, we say so in the description following their listing, and let you know how well they supply. Many new suppliers have sprung up in the last few years; we have only sent away for their catalogues. Most of them are studios themselves, which have expanded into the supplier category. More will open up by the time this book is printed; you can find out about them by subscribing to one of the glass journals listed below, particularly *Stained Glass Journal,* or by consulting the Yellow Pages under "Stained and Leaded Glass."

Before you start sending off to these national suppliers, we want to recommend first that you try three alternatives. First, always try your local craft store, or the crafts section of a local department store; they have the capital and the know-how to stock your supplies if you ask them to. Second, try locating any local stained glass artists; they may be willing to sell you supplies, as well as help instruct you. These artists include new ones and the old ones; both usually list themselves in the *Yellow Pages* under "Stained Glass." Third, try your local glass company, or a glass company in a nearby city; they are also in a position to stock art glass and glass tools if they do not already. Many stores need only to be convinced that the interest is around to invest in tools and supplies.

From these three local, immediate sources, you should find enough materials to work with right from the start. You'll also be able to see firsthand what you are buying. You may pay twice what you will eventually pay, if you decide to continue in glass, but the difference between $5 and $10, or $25 and $50, at this stage of the game should be negligible compared to the hundreds of dollars you may spend later on.

Glass

Accessibility to a good supply of colored art glass of all kinds has probably been the number one obstacle to reviving the so-called "lost art" of stained glass. The glass has been carefully used and purchased within the structure of large, traditional stained glass studios and large, traditional suppliers; first they were American studios and European manufacturers, and now they are American studios and American manufacturers. The new entrant into the field, the individual glassworker, has been faced with dealing only with second- or third-hand

152

sources, retail houses where you can only buy broken bits of glass by the pound. There used to be two glass houses in New York City importing and selling European glass to the smaller buyer; now, with the closing of Leo Popper and Sons, there is only one. Generally, the little guys are forced to think of such radical alternatives as making their own glass, making the most out of scrap glass, or switching to another medium.

Fortunately, with the tremendous increase in demand for glass, more suppliers have opened up. There is even a glass company which opened recently, expressly for the purpose of supplying the new glass artists (see "Colorado Art Glass" below). We have researched the market extensively, and for the first time in print we can present as complete a listing of suppliers and manufacturers of glass as you'll find anywhere.

We recommend that you explore the three alternatives outlined above—craft store, glass artists, and glass companies—as well as look into three other possibilities. One, find old clear glass. It is available everywhere: in old barns, in junkyards, in decaying window sashes. It has streaks, bubbles, and greenish tints. As an artist, you are a natural recycler. Two, as you develop, see if any local or regional glassblower would be interested in making you sheet glass, however small and irregular, from the batches of glass he uses for blowing art pieces. Three, before setting your sights on fantastic, large, glass-consuming projects, think small: with a light box, a tool and glass box, and a 4 foot by 4 foot space, you could turn out an endless supply of nice lamps. You can make mold lamps or boxes out of small pieces of scrap glass, the throwaways of large studios or manufacturers (see

"Kokomo Glass Company" below). You could use these same small pieces in your leaded windows; just use smaller, thinner lead and more intricate designs.

Mail-Order Retail Houses

• Whittemore-Durgin Glass Company (also called "Stained Glass of Hanover"), Box 2065, Hanover, Mass. 02339 (617-871-1790). The oldest mail-order stained glass business in the country; they gear themselves to the "hobbyist," with a very chatty, busy catalogue. They supply all kinds of glass, sold by the pound, usually in remnant (throwaway) forms. Catalogue available on request.

• Nervo Studios, 2027 7th Street, Berkeley, Cal. 94710. Like W-D, a studio which produces its own stained glass products, and which has expanded into supplying glass and tools. They sell European and American cathedrals and antiques, but do not sell American opalescent. Like some other suppliers, they have switched to European (Belgium) and Asian (Vietnamese) opalescents, since there is such a backordering of American opalescent. Very orderly catalogue, covering same range of tools and jewels as W-D. They sell their glass by the sheet (roughly 2 feet by 3 feet) and not in scrap form.

• The Stained Glass Club, Box 244, Norwood, N.J. 07648. Another studio which grew into a supplier. For a $10 membership fee, you can buy their glass and tools and supplies at a discount (10 to 20 percent). They sell their glass in precut, 6 inch by 5 inch minisheets. You can also buy from them without becoming a member. Catalogue costs one dollar.

• Coran-Sholes Industries, 509 E. Second Street, South Boston, Mass. 02027 (617-268-3780). Basically a lead and solder supplier, C-S has begun selling a limited range of cathedrals, antiques, and opalescents. They are cut in half-sheet sizes of 32 inches by 42 inches. They also sell remnants. Glass is sent via UPS, and C-S may cut sheets to size in order to ship. Larger sheets are available when picked up.

• S. A. Bendheim, 122 Hudson Street, New York, N.Y. 10013 (212-226-6370). The only glass importer in the country that we know of that will sell small orders (under $200). They sell American opalescents in precut (3 square foot) sheets downstairs, and a wide range of imported cathedrals and antiques on the upper three floors. They also carry American cathedrals. Sample cases are available, for a charge, on request. Full sheets can either be cut down and sent via UPS, or packed and crated and sent via commercial trucking. There are order limitations for each category — opalescent, cathedral, antique — when mail-ordering. Any quantity is available when picked up. They also sell a wide range of jewels, rondels, and *dalles,* as well as lead and glass tools.

"Pick Up Only"
Retail Outlets

• "The Op Shop," Kokomo Opalescent Glass Company, 1310 S. Market Street, Kokomo, Ind. 46901. This is the retail outlet of Kokomo Glass, which is perhaps the most prestigious opalescent glass maker in the world. Kokomo sells only to the large studios in the trade, and to other large architectural accounts. Through the "Op Shop" they make scraps — irregular breaks and cut-offs — available to the individual craftsman or hobbyist. We have had good luck using these scraps in detailing windows, in mold lamps, and for small projects such as jewelry boxes. Plan to spend a few hours digging through the many barrels of broken glass; they sell it by the pound, and supply you with gloves. "The Op Shop" also sells glass tools and supplies and selected lamps of some of the best glassworkers around the country.

• San Francisco Stained Glass Works, 3463 16th Street, San Francisco, Cal. 94114. They are a mail-order house when it comes to tools and lamp molds. They will not send glass, however. They carry a full range of European and American antique, opalescent, and cathedrals, as well as jewels and *dalles*. Their catalogue is available on request.

Wholesale Glass Importers

• Bienenfeld Industries, Inc., 1541 Covert St., Brooklyn, N.Y. 11227 (212-821-4400). They advertise the same range of imported glasses, opalescents, *dalles*, and rondels as does S. A. Bendheim. The one difference is the $15 charge for samples, and the minimum order of $200.

• C & R Loo, Importers of German Glass, 6221 Holles Street, Emeryville, Cal. 94662. We saw them listed in *Glass Art Magazine*; that is all.

• Whittemore-Durgin Glass Company, 107 Trumbull Street, Elizabeth, N.J. 07206 (201-352-0100). Please note that this address is different from the one listed earlier. This is W-D's warehouse, where they sell minimum orders of $50 and up on a first-come-first-served basis. Whenever they receive a new shipment, they send out a price list to their wholesale accounts. Write for more information.

Glass Manufacturers

We list here American manufacturers only, as no one except the importers deals directly with the European manufacturers. When you get to this stage, you may wish to write to these manufacturers to find out their representatives in your area of the country. You are talking about a minimum order of at least one crate (400 square feet) of glass, which can take over a year in delivery. The first of these companies, you will note, currently sells in smaller case lots, but they, too, will be upping their minimum order, while simultaneously lowering their prices.

• Colorado Art Glass Works, 1516 Blake Street, Denver, Col. 80202. These people are starting a new business, just when the older ones are saying that the cost of fuel and materials is almost unbearable. They are making sheets (roughly 3 square feet each) of glass, last seen when Tiffany Studios were in operation. Streaky opals, chalky opalescents, unusual cathedrals, and a variety of blown shades, tiles, jewels, and rondels are what they sell. Their colors so far have varied with each new batch, even though they send out samples for you to order by. They advertise in all the craft and glass journals and are eager to be supported by the individual, contemporary glass artist. Their glass costs more than that of the other manufacturers, but they will open new accounts and do supply a unique glass. New kilns will lower their costs, and by ordering a case of one color you can lower the cost even more.

• Blenko Glass Company, Milton, W. V. 25541. Many serious glass artists we know make annual trips to Blenko, either to purchase sheet antique or *dalles*. If you order by mail, Blenko will not send samples, as they make so many colors and variations. If you visit their factory, you can see how the antique sheets are made, thanks to an informative factory tour, open free of charge to the public. Blenko antique is more wavy and dappled than European antique and is very easy to cut. This is the only glass company in America making antique sheet glass and *dalles*.

• Kokomo Opalescent Glass Company, 1310 S. Market Street, Kokomo, Ind. 46901. A supplier in opalescent glass to the trade since 1888. (See above.)

• The Paul Wissmach Glass Company, Paden City, W. Va. 26159. Write to find your area representatives. They manufacture fine opalescents and cathedral glasses and are unable to meet the tremendous demand for these; like Kokomo, they generally sell to old, established accounts, and if you are able to place an order through one of their representatives, you may have to wait over a year for delivery.

• The Advance Glass Company, Newark, O. 43055. They make cathedral and opalescent glasses, and will sell directly to wholesale accounts only.

Lead

For small quantities (sold by the strip, rather than by boxes of 25 pounds or more), try any of the retail glass houses listed above, except for Coran-Sholes Industries in Boston. Again, too, try your local craft shop, glass company, or stained glass artist.

For quantities of 25 pounds and up, try Coran-Sholes Industries (see above for address); they have 35 styles of lead and are the only supplier we know of dealing at this level. They supply quickly, in 6 foot cardboard boxes, via UPS.

For large-quantity orders (100 pounds and up), try any of the following suppliers:

• Gardiner Metal Company (minimum of 130 pounds), 4820 S. Campbell Ave., Chicago, Ill. 60632. One hundred styles to choose from.

• White Metal Rolling and Stamping Corp., 80 Moultrie St., Brooklyn, N.Y. 11222 (minimum of 100 pounds, or two orders of 50 pounds). One hundred ten styles to choose from.

• Crown Metal Company, 117 E. Washington Street, Milwaukee, Wis. 53204.

• Quemetco Inc., 2700 16th Ave. SW, Seattle, Wash. 98134. 115 styles.

• G. A. Arvil Co., Lead Products Division, Box 12050, Cincinnati, O. 45212.

Solder

In a pinch, you can try your local hardware store; they

sometimes carry both 50–50 percent and 60–40 per-cent solder in half-pound quantities, for electrical hobby use. If you can only get 50–50 percent, you can use a hotter soldering iron, such as a soldering gun, and a stronger flux for your leadwork, such as Nokorode Soldering Paste (which we have recommended above only for copper foil work). Otherwise, try the following:

• Any of the retail glass houses listed above.

• White Metal, Gardiner Metal, and Crown Metal (see above, under "Lead").

• Check around; there may be a metals company near you making solder; we have heard of such companies, where you can buy your solder in spools of 25 to 50 pounds, at a substantial saving.

Copper Foil

We have noted differences in quality of solder from one manufacturer to another; the same is especially true of copper foil. Some appears to be made solely for glass artists, while other name brands are electrical tape, used commercially and professionally by many kinds of people. The first kind is murky-looking, seems tinted, and is often thick, and therefore tends to cut you as you work with it. The second kind is bright and shiny, and comes sealed from the factory and not in a stapled plastic Baggie. This is the kind of foil we buy: in our case, directly from a factory outlet of the 3M (Minnesota Mining and Manufacturing) Company of St. Paul, Minnesota. They market their tape under the Scotch Tape label, call it "Electrical Conducting Tape," and wrap four rolls to a single core of cardboard. You peel away paper from the back of the tape to expose the adhesive, whereas with lesser-quality tapes the adhesive is not protected. Mystik Tape Company also makes copper foil tape, under the "Borden" label. All these companies, when ordering direct, will require a minimum order. If you have to buy the roll from your supplier, make sure you are getting the most for your money; if the tape has a brand label on the inside core, you can be usually assured that it will do the job well.

Lead and Solder Colorants

We finish our leaded work with a homemade putty described above; we add *lamp black*, commonly sold in hardware or paint stores, to the portland cement, whiting, plaster of paris, and linseed oil, all of which can be bought through your hardware store or building supplier. A more old-fashioned treatment of lead and solder is *gun blue*, a chemical sold at hardware stores for use on gun barrels, which cleans and grays a barrel, and leaves a smooth gray-black surface when applied to lead calms.

With copper foiled work, a variety of colorants is available. Generally you begin with *copper sulfate crystals*, which all stained glass suppliers carry. When simply mixed with water the crystals produce a splotchy brown-to-copper color on the solder, giving the lampshade an "antiqued" look. For a darker, pewter finish, you can mix *household ammonia*, commonly sold at grocery stores, with the crystals. If you heat the mixture, the color will appear more quickly, as the solution will be more active. Also, you can add *tinner's fluid*, sold at your hardware store, to the crystals to produce this dark, pewter-like finish; it contains a portion of hydrofluoric acid.

If you are not interested in experimenting with your own solutions, Nervo Studios offer both a "Copper Patina" and a "Black Patina" for finishing soldered surfaces, as well as for plating old lamp bases. See above for their address.

Other Metals

We need to use other metals besides lead and copper foil. We need steel for barring windows, zinc calm for hanging heavy cylinder bottoms, and copper channel for finishing the bottom edges of copper-foiled lampshades.

We are lucky enough to buy our steel bars (either ⅜ inch round, or ⅜ inch or ½ inch flat) from a local blacksmith, who in turn buys them from a rolled steel supplier in our area. You ought to pursue this sort of avenue for your bars. If not, larger steel suppliers, like White Metal

Rolling and Stamping Corp. (see above), will send you the bars you want. Usually this is not an item you will want to stock up on to a great extent; with such materials as Plexiglas around (see Jack Trompetter's reinforcing diagram), barring windows is possibly going to become a bit obsolete. Of course, this will add more authenticity to a restoration window, and the cost of three bars versus a full sheet of Plexiglas is quite different.

For zinc calm and copper channel, the best supplier we have found is: Chicago Metallic Corp., 4849 S. Austin Ave., Chicago, Ill. 60638. Write and they will send you a catalogue and ordering information.

Tools

These essential items wll be carried by all the retail glass houses described above; each varies in delivery time, and each carries different kinds of cutters, lead knives, grozers, and soldering irons. Both Coran Sholes and Whittemore-Durgin carry the Esico 60-watt iron we have recommended; Esico is located in Deep River, Connecticut, and therefore markets well in this region. Many of the others carry Weller irons, and other brand names. If you cannot get an Esico #9460 locally, you can write Esico (Electric Soldering Iron Company) and ask where they sell their irons near you. Otherwise, you can deal with C–S or W–D. For speed, we have had our best luck with C–S. With the other tools, try to handle any of the tools before you order one; this would mean visiting a local studio or glass artist's shop, or driving to the supplier rather than ordering by mail. Lead knives vary in weight and feel, as do glass cutters. Perhaps you will not worry about these intangibles until you are more accomplished.

Rare Tools

Diamond Cutter

(excellent for repetitive cuts, especially on clear glass) — find a traveling salesman, as Barbara did many years ago (her diamond cutter is still working, with the warning, however, that once it is used by one person, no one else should use it, or the diamond may pop out), or from the prompt and efficient Brookstone Company, Peterborough, N. H. 03458.

Vibrating Pencil

(for engraving your name into your work) — write Burgess Vibrocrafters, Inc., Grayslake, Ill. 60030; you will need a special carbide tip, which they carry. The body of the vibrating pencil is sold in many hardware stores, such as the Aubuchon chain in the Northeast; the carbide tip has to be sent away for, however.

Kilns and Kiln Materials

For a kiln, check with your local or area potters' supply house. What you are looking for is a front-loading electric kiln, with a thermostat and pyrometer, at least 18 inches deep and tall. Top-loaders are not preferred, as they vent the heat when opened to inspect the glass during the firing. You may be able to find a used electric kiln, the product of an overzealous beginner in pottery, which should cost around $100. You can also build your own kiln: the best way to do this is to first read *The Kiln Book*, written by internationally-known potter Frederick L. Olsen, and published by Keramos Books, a division of Westwood Potters Supply in Los Angeles (first published in 1973). His final chapter describes how to make your own electric kiln, for a substantial saving over buying one commercially.

For mold material, you can buy the *gauging plaster* or *plaster of paris* recommended by Stephen Schneider at a hardware or building supply store. For refireable mold material, order; *Visal Castable* (HW13-65) in 100-pound lots, from Harbison-Walker Company, 2 Gateway Center, Pittsburgh, Pa. 15322. For *stains* and *paints*, try your retail glass supplier, or deal directly with: L. Reusche and Company, 2–6 Lister Avenue, Newark, N.J. 07105. The also sell the *badger brushes* you'll need. (Quoting Jack Trompetter: "They are an old respectable company; they take their time and won't be rushed. Will send samples for fifty cents but ask for a minimum order of ten bucks.")

For actual painted and fired glass panels, for collectors or dealers, or for your own enjoyment, write: Glass Masters, 110 W. 7th St., New York, N.Y. 10011. They will send you a color catalogue of their contemporary painted work.

Acids

• Hydrofluoric acid—for etching flashed glass (see Jack Trompetter, Chapter Five). Try Farrell Chemicals, Burlington, Vt. 05401. The latest prices were $18 per gallon retail, $5 per gallon for lots of 25 gallons or more, and successively cheaper in larger lots. As Jack Trompetter recommends: "Buy cooperatively and you'll get an easier deal from them. Give them a rap about your stained glass work and that'll help too."

• Muriatic (hydrochloric) acid—for cleaning old lamp bases, for removing the metallic backing on costume jewelry jewels—Nervo Studios (see above) lists this in their catalogue; other suppliers may start to also. Also, ask your local druggist if he can order it for you.

• Oleic acid—for fluxing lead and solder. Sold at all retail glass suppliers, and also through your local druggist (sometimes).

• Nokorode Soldering Paste—for fluxing copper foil and

solder, and also for use on lead (a stronger flux than oleic acid, yet harder to clean up). Sold in hardware stores everywhere. Also in larger, one-pound cans, by some retail glass suppliers. Consult their catalogues.

Lamp Bases

This is a tough one. Barbara and I constantly argue about old versus new bases. She makes reproduction shades, and likes putting them on old bases she buys at junk stores all around the country (we have had the best luck, lately, in upstate New York). Yet I find the bases too old-looking to put a new old lampshade on. The solution, of course, may be to have the old bases *plated*; this means finding a company nearby which can dip your bases; usually this is done best in a batch of many bases at once.

The other route to follow is the production of new bases, along the lines of the old ones. Whittemore-Durgin, Nervo Studios, and a lamp parts supplier we know of advertise reproduction bases; we have never bought one (we've often asked and they have not had them in stock); we assumed they have their own molds and make their own bases. Bauer and Coble Studios, located near the University of Illinois, Champaign-Urbana, have a friend at the university who casts their exquisite molds for them, along the exact lines of the bases that original Tiffany lampshades sat upon.

In keeping with this line of pursuit is the idea of making bases out of other materials, particularly clay. We work close to a group of potters, and the idea has often occurred to the more contemporary-minded of us (me) to commission one of these potters to throw a few experimental forms, with a solid glaze fired under oxidation. We have also talked of having woodworkers lathe a base for us. Barbara contends that glass looks good only on metal bases, and that anything else will detract from the glass-and-metal shade. Try and see what you think, if you have a mind to.

Lamp Parts

Over the years, we have had the best luck with a local electrical supply store. They can help you select the odd pieces you need for each shade you make. On the other hand, if you can order from a wholesale electrical parts supplier in your area, you can save substantially on wiring, sockets, brass fittings, and chain. If neither of these avenues interests you, your national mail-order glass retailers all carry electrical lamp parts, and they can help you out. It really helps in wiring, however, actually to see the parts you need, and this is why your local lamp parts store (even some of the larger hardware stores carry all the parts) can be so helpful.

Lamp Shade Holder

This is an invaluable tool, a bracketed arm affair, fully adjustable, which will hold your shade at the necessary angle when you are trying to float it. Otherwise you often burn yourself, holding the shade in your lap. We have never succeeded in locating one. Whittemore-Durgin and Nervo Studios now both advertise them, and an old flyer from Franciscan Arts, 100 San Antonio Circle, Mountain View, California 94040, advertised this company as a direct supplier of lamp shade holders. Write them and see if they are still in business, and then you'll be in business, too.

Lamp Molds

Louis Tiffany could afford to have artisans hand-lathe the molds he used out of wood; these were heavy and lasted indefinitely. In this age of plastic, it is natural that we would have plastic molds. Whittemore-Durgin sells a wood-pulp mold, which we have never seen. Coran-Sholes sells the H. L. Worden (of Box 519, Granger, Washington 98932) "Modular Shade Forms," which are 1/6 sections of Styrofoam molds, encouraging you to design one pattern which can be repeated six times and then joined to make a full form. Finally, San

Francisco Stained Glass Works, like W-D, sells a full line of Styrofoam molds.

Lamp Patterns

Whittemore-Durgin has reproduced many of the more famous Tiffany lampshade patterns. They list them in their catalogue. You can check a book of Tiffany lamps (see below, "Recommended Reading") to see the pattern you like, and then order it.

H. L. Worden, with their Modular Shade Forms (see above), have patterns of several dozen shades cut to fit their forms; Coran-Sholes Industries is their Eastern representative, or you could write H. L. Worden (see above) for the name of a representative near you.

Recommended Reading

Books

Designs and Patterns from Historic Ornament (formerly titled *Outlines of Ornament in the Leading Styles*), by W. and G. Audsley, Dover Publications, New York, 1968.

Handmade Houses: A Guide to the Woodbutcher's Art, by Art Boericke and Barry Shapiro, Scrimshaw Press, San Francisco, 1973. This book could also be called "a guide to the glassworker's art." Many of these marvelous handmade houses have original windows, California style, and old stained glass windows, reused in the most imaginative and sensuous of ways. The book *in toto* gives celebration to the fact that the Woodstock Generation did exist, and did raise monuments—human-scaled—to its moment in time.

Stained Glass Craft, by J. A. F. Divine and G. Blachford, Dover Press, New York, 1972. This is a reprint of a book originally published in 1940. It is a handy black and white, compact description of the European practices of painting, leading, and glazing. Patrick Reyntiens's book (see below) is a much longer version of these techniques, with color photographs, for a substantially higher pricetag.

Art Glass Nouveau, by Ray and Lee Grover, Charles E. Tuttle Co., Rutland, Vt. 424 color plates of art nouveau glass.

Woodstock Handmade Houses, by Robert Haney and David Ballantine, photographs by Jonathan Elliot, Random House, New York, 1974. This is the East Coast's answer to California's *Handmade Houses* (see above). Remember, Woodstock is where "Woodstock Generation" began. Interesting to note the aesthetic differences (if any) and the uses of glass in the two regions. A good book; nicely complements its predecessor.

An Idea Book of Stained Glass Lampshade Designs, compiled by James H. Hepburn, President Press, Milton, Mass., 1972. Available through Whittemore-Durgin (see "Suppliers").

An Idea Book of Victorian and Art Nouveau Stained Glass Window Designs, compiled by James H. Hepburn, President Press, 1973. Available through Whittemore-Durgin.

Creating Stained Glass Lampshades, by James H. Hepburn, President Press, 1974. Available through Whittemore-Durgin.

Louis Comfort Tiffany, Rebel in Glass, by Robert Koch, Crown Publications, New York, 1964. Good biography material on the great man.

Art and Stained Glass, by Claude Lips, Doubleday, Garden City, N. Y., 1973. Good description on how to lead up a window; nothing, however, about copper foil work.

The Stained Glass Windows of Chagall, 1957–70, by Robert Marteau, Tudor Publications, New York, 1973. Seven churches, in Europe and the United States, with Chagall's painted windows.

Lamps of Tiffany, by Dr. Egon Neustadt, Fairfield Press, New York. This book is so incredible you cannot believe it is a book. A visual, handheld cinema of Tiffany shades you would not believe, grouped according to kind. All in color and beautifully done. Something to work hard to afford (it costs $135).

The Techniques of Stained Glass, by Patrick Reyntiens, Watson-Guptill, New York, 1967. This is *the* book on painting and firing on glass, and is a virtual glass-worker's Bible. Complete description of how to set up a professional studio along century-old lines. Humble, complete, the quintessence of the European traditions in stained glass.

Craft and Glass Publications

Glass Art Magazine, bi-monthly, $15. Box 7527, Oakland, Calif. 94601. The first of its kind, a journal for blown and leaded glass. Now in its third year. With an annual slide competition (those selected by its jury are printed, in color or black and white), and rental of these slides is available. Some listing of suppliers, and articles on contemporary glassworkers.

Stained Glass Journal, the quarterly magazine of the Stained Glass Association of America, 1125 Wilmington Ave., St. Louis, Mo. 63111. $8.00 per year. You can also become a member of this organization (we are not), after a selection process, and by paying a fee be listed in the magazine. Articles are usually tributes to the best work of the member studios, giving a traditional viewpoint on stained glass work in America. Excellent listing of glass and material suppliers, particularly for the beginner.

Craft Horizons Magazine, the magazine of the American Crafts Council, 44 W. 53rd St., New York 10019. $12.50 and up, depending upon the kind of membership you select in the ACC. Articles on all media, with some recent listing of glass suppliers. A good look at other people working in other media. Membership in the ACC makes you eligible for ACC-sponsored fairs in your region (ACC has five regional offices).